Praise for The Love Yourself Dare

"*The Love Yourself Dare* is absolutely a must read for those who have lost themselves in the triangle of love. It will restore hope and bring tears to your eyes as you engage yourself in this beautiful message. The author has a way of pulling you in and making you feel as if you are actually there with her, recalling the happenings and events in her life. May this message change the past, the present, and even the course of your future, as you come to understand and recognize your life path and the important call you have to "Embrace your Place."

~ Carol Ann Guest, Mrs. Utah America 2011 & Founder of "Embrace your Place"

"As a guy, I found this is a gripping read. Jennifer's stories made me reflect on my own marriage and how I treat my wife. Her insight helped me reflect on my actions and thoughts, and how they affect my relationship. You can't read this book and not think about how to strengthen your relationship with your spouse."

~Jason Alba, Author & Professional Speaker

"*The Love Yourself Dare* is a shining real-life example of how possible it is to experience new beginnings at any stage of life. With heart wrenching honesty and heartwarming insight into challenges so many women can relate to, this book gives readers a glimpse of the capacity we all have to spark a transformation in ourselves from weakness to strength. Jennifer's story shows the beauty of letting pain—awful, dark, seemingly unbearable pain—become a catalyst for promising change and marvelous growth."

~Lindsay Kite, Co-Founder & Owner of Beauty Redefined

"Jennifer Griffiths Manges has written an extraordinary book—beautiful, moving and honest. Most important, she gives us a practical way to learn to start honoring ourselves again. This book can change your life."

~Kim Flynn, Speaker, Trainer & Business Consultant

"This authentically written book will help you understand that loving yourself is a journey and a process. In *The Love Yourself Dare*, Jennifer's story exposed my own vulnerability as I took a second look at what it REALLY means to love yourself! The combination of raw & relevant compelled me to finish it in one sitting!"

~Ann Webb, Life Vision Expert & Trainer

"Jennifer Griffiths Manges has written a wise and insightful book that sheds a bright beam of hope on individual worth. With tender vulnerability, Jennifer shares her deeply personal journey through self-betrayal, self-awareness and self-empowerment. I highly recommend *The Love Yourself Dare* to anyone who wants practical ways to begin breaking through personal barriers to enjoy a life of freedom and joy."

~Cherie Burton, Purpose, Speaking and Image Coach

"*The Love Yourself Dare* is a fabulous story about one woman's search for love and perfection. You'll find a heart-wrenching story about her struggles and the sacrifices she made to hold her family and marriage together, something she held sacred. You'll be compelled to keep reading and you'll be amazed at the strength that can come from within a person when she finally learns to love herself."

~ Shanna Beaman, Author, Professional speaker and Trainer

"This is not just another 'feel good', fluffy self-help! The author shows you her personal journey as she wrestled with the dark times and walks you through inspired thoughts and skills to battle the same darkness everyone fights every day! Truly a gift to women and the men who love them!"

~Kaisie Alba, Songwriter

"Jennifer Griffiths Manges has written a wonderfully powerful and inspiring book, *The Love Yourself Dare*. It's about how to truly love and accept yourself. Women and girls of all ages can embrace and become empowered by reading it. It's an excellent way to get a daily dose of inspiration and healing for your body, mind and spirit. It's a beautiful journey about how magical and healing the power of self-love really is. It is deeply transformational, this is a book you will cherish and enjoy for years to come."

~Carol Whitaker, Lifestyle, Fitness & Life Success Coach

"Absolutely inspirational! The author has taken a very challenging life experience and used it to not only strengthen herself, but to teach us all how to gracefully overcome life's obstacles. Each page opened my mind to new and better ways of living a physically, emotionally, and spiritually balanced life. This is a must read!"

~Christi Dickerson, Homemaker

"I read this book from cover to cover and all in the same day. *The Love Yourself Dare* is a life-changing book about finding yourself, becoming real, and discovering the beauty that is within you. My life has been changed because of Jennifer's story. *The Love Yourself Dare* will touch your heart as you learn to love yourself and enjoy all of life's endless possibilities."

~Lindy Kerby, Inspirational songwriter

"*The Love Yourself Dare* is Jennifer Griffiths Manges' real-life journey from losing herself to loving herself. This inspirational story shows the strength of the human spirit in overcoming difficulties—both big and small—and it is one book you will think about long after you've closed the last page."

~Julie Coulter Bellon, Author of Ribbon of Darkness

"Jennifer Griffiths Manges knows how to share—with honesty and courage. If life has kicked you in the stomach and you wonder if you can heal and learn to care for yourself, then Jennifer's story will shout a resounding YES to you. This book can change your life!"

~Mary Ann Johnson, Home School coach

The Love Yourself Dare

One Woman's Journey from Self-Loathing to Self-Love

Jennifer Griffiths Manges

"The Love Yourself Dare" by Jennifer Griffiths Manges

Copyright © 2012 by Jennifer Griffiths Manges

Published in the United States of America by SOULutions, LLC

Cover Photos: Hands in Chains with Butterfly © istockphoto.com/Amanda Rohde

Crown © istockphoto.com/Ivan Burmistrov

Cover design: Jennifer Griffiths Manges

All Rights Reserved. No part of this publication may be reproduced, stored in a retrieval system or transmitted in any form or by any means, electronic, mechanical, photocopy, recording device or otherwise without prior written permission from the author.

This book is designed to provide an account of personal experience. The information is given with the understanding that neither the author nor publisher is engaged in rendering legal or professional advice. As the details of each individual situation are subjective, you should seek additional advice and the services of competent professionals in the field that meets your needs.

For more information visit: www.TheLoveYourselfDare.com

ISBN 978-0-9853790-0-1

Dedication

This book is dedicated to my daughter,
A beautiful light in my life.
And
To every woman or girl who
has ever felt unworthy, ugly or unloved,
and is ready to know the truth about her own
beauty and worth.

Acknowledgments

This book was a huge undertaking for me and could not have been accomplished without the love and support of some incredible people:

~Thank you, Peggy Keller, for believing in me and my story. Your credibility in the industry and your generosity in sharing information gave me the courage to sit down and begin writing.

~Jason Alba, you were the perfect mentor. Without your generous guidance I would likely have stalled during the writing process and *The Love Yourself Dare* would not be in the hands of readers for many years to come. Thank you for your kindness and believing in this project enough to sacrifice your time to it.

~Thank you, Darlene Craven Michaelis, for your swift and professional work and for making my words shine. Your flexibility and support on this project were invaluable.

~My ex-husband, you know who you are. Without you there would be no story to tell. I am grateful that we have finally found peace between us.

~To my parents, Jim and Connie Neilson, words cannot express the gratitude I feel for both the childcare you provided and the roof over my head during the writing and transitional phases of my life. I will be forever grateful for your love, support and belief in me.

~To Barry Manges, the love of my life. Your gentleness, sensitivity, and patience continue to astound me. You are my sounding board, my voice of reason, my shoulder to cry on, my angel and my best friend. Your unconditional love and belief in me heal my heart in new ways every day. I am honored to call you my husband.

~My children, thank you for always believing in me and still thinking I'm "cool", even when I feel like a failure. You are the light and joy of my life. Your strength and courage to be who you are despite what anyone else says or thinks is a constant inspiration to me. You are amazing!

~And finally, thank you God. Thank you for every heartache and pain, for every lesson and healed wound that has allowed me to write this story. Thank you for forgiveness and the gift of new beginnings. Thank you for opportunities to grow and the valuable lesson that with hard work come rewards. For the knowledge gained and the triumphs won, no matter the size, I am truly and eternally grateful.

The Love Yourself Dare

One Woman's Journey from Self-Loathing to Self-Love

Jennifer Griffiths Manges

Table of Contents

Book I

A Rapid Merger 1

Underdeveloped Roots 3

The Business of Blending 5

Little Rejections 9

Settling In 11

The List of Devastation 13

Changes 17

Contention Rising 19

Desert Bloom 21

A Seed Planted 23

World Upside Down 25

Book II

Soul Cleaning 29

Sitting with the Enemy 31

Bedroom Woes 33

An Unusual Drug 35

Permission to Pretend 37

Breaking through Walls 39

Another Haunting Thought 43

The Pit of Hell 45

Attempt at Easy 47

Surprises and Pain 49

Dark Addiction Revealed 53

Life-Altering Decision 55

Fearing People's Opinions 57

Faltering 59

Interview 61

Into the Lion's Den 63

Understanding 67

Book III

Missed Opportunity 71

Unrest Rising 73

Pain in the Silence 77

The Caterpillar's Dilemma 81

Sunset by the Sea 83

Remembering How to Breathe 89

The Gift of Space 93

Shifting Focus 97

Observing Beauty 101

Fish Back in Water 103

Gentle Lessons 107

Ebb and Flow 111

An End and a Beginning 113

Book IV

White Flag 117

The Lines We Draw 121

Gone 123

Dream of Death 125

Another Decision 127

Separation by Degrees 129

Mirrors 131

Backing Out 133

Freedom Behind Bars 135

The Gift of Beauty and Release 139

Transformation in White 143

Tiny Crown 147

Be Who You Are 149

Daring to Live and Love 153

About the Dares 157

The Dares

Dare 1: It's All About Desire 159

Dare 2: The Importance of Awareness 163

Dare 3: Lighten Up 165

Dare 4: Record It 167

Dare 5: What's Water Got to Do With It? 169

Dare 6: Love Withholds Judgment 171

Dare 7: Love Allows 175

Dare 8: Love Breathes 177

Dare 9: Body Mapping 179

Dare 10: Beliefs and Perceptions 183

Dare 11: Belief Hunt on Beauty 187

Dare 12: Drug of Choice 191

Dare 13: Belief Hunt on Worthiness 193

Dare 14: Healing and Time 195

Dare 15: I AM 197

Dare 16: Journaling 199

Dare 17: Personality Profile 201

Dare 18: Talent and Gift Inventory 203

Dare 19: Alignment 205

Dare 20: Stillness 209

Dare 21: Nutrition 211

Dare 22: Stress Management 213

Dare 23: Safety and Boundaries 217

Dare 24: Balance 219

Dare 25: Coloring Feelings 221

Dare 26: Symbolism of Desires 223

Dare 27: Gratitude 225

Dare 28: Creation and Creativity 227

Dare 29: Question Power 229

Dare 30: Whose Fault Is It? 231

Dare 31: Order 235

Dare 32: Physical Beauty 237

Dare 33: Fear vs. Courage 239

Dare 34: Self-Betrayal 241

Dare 35: Basic Body Language 243

Dare 36: Life Vision 245

Dare 37: Nourishment 247

Dare 38: Solutions 249

Dare 39: Rhythm 251

Dare 40: Self-Expression 253

Dare 41: Freedom 255

Dare 42: Social Interaction 257

Dare 43: Beauty Hunt 259

Dare 44: Mirroring 261

Dare 45: The Gift of You 265

Introduction

In an effort to respect personal privacy, I have changed the names of everyone involved in this story.

It is an intricate task to look back on a relationship and try to convey the truth. There are always two sides to every story. I have tried, as much as possible, to share MY story, but because it was created with another person I have had to share some of the details of OUR story. My intent has never been to disparage the man who helped me create this story. In fact, I am deeply grateful for all I have learned from him, for the circumstances our relationship created that taught me the lessons I needed to learn to become a better person, and to be endowed with the experiences that would allow me to serve others with greater compassion.

This story is told through my eyes—through the lenses of my perception—from where I was mentally and emotionally at the time of each experience. For you to understand my loss and subsequent victory, I must include something of the sorrow I lived by sharing personal details with you. It is my wish that you recognize that neither my ex-spouse nor I are the same people we were when this story took place. That is the miracle of letting go, forgiveness and change. Because of this miracle, I feel this story can safely be shared with you in the spirit of hope that it will give you the strength and permission to love yourself and move beyond whatever prisons or challenges you are experiencing in your life at this time. May my past struggle and heartaches bolster you in your own difficulties. Know that healing is possible, as are forgiveness and love, even towards those whom we feel have hurt us the most. When we release ourselves to change, we allow others around us to change as well.

With that, I share this very personal account of devastation, reclamation and love with you.

Book I

The Subtle Descent to Hell

A Rapid Merger

Exhilaration.
That's what I felt when he was around.
Passion.
That's what I felt when we kissed.
And kiss we did. In fact, that's almost all we did. Making out was the hallmark of our relationship. We were two sets of lips and the people attached to them were the appendages. I didn't care though. It felt good to be loved and desired.

He was four years older than I. Independent, well-dressed and smooth as honey, he was a real charmer. I was a senior in high school, naïve in many ways, and completely swept away by his dark hair and chocolate eyes that smoldered beneath thick black lashes. I'd always been a sucker for the tall, dark and handsome type and when he looked at me, my heart not only skipped a beat, it went to an entirely different planet.

He was my first real boyfriend. I'd never given guys much time. Certainly I'd given them plenty of attention, but I was generally afraid of relationships as a teenager. When he came along though, all my fears melted away like ice cream under hot syrup. He said he loved me and told me I was beautiful. He bought me roses and perfume. He did everything right to sweep a young romantic girl off her feet, and I fell madly in love.

I was eighteen.

By the time things got serious, about a month into our relationship, I decided I wanted to go away to college, experience life, date around a little bit.

He wanted to get married.

There were tears and arguments—not disagreements, but weepy, unsettling arguments that left him pouting on my front lawn and me wrestling with feelings of guilt. Finally, I ended the struggle by agreeing to get married. And we did, exactly six months after our first date. I loved him. He was a great guy; so talented, so competent, so strong, with a body that knocked my socks off. We had nothing in common except our religious denomination and an undeniable physical attraction. And being so young, I didn't know what I wanted in life, or the type of personality in a marriage partner that would best compliment me. The only thing I really knew was that I wanted to be a wife and mother one day so I put my dreams of a higher education on hold and got married.

Matt, my new fiancé, had a mother that was concerned about the speed of our engagement. My parents were totally comfortable with it, having experienced their own whirlwind courtship 25 years earlier. I was a mix of emotions, but once I made the decision to marry, I never looked back. I completely surrendered to love. Staring into my future husband's enchanting gaze so full of promise, possibility and love, I smiled with delight, trusting (as most young couples do) that we would be happy and everything would be wonderful.

Underdeveloped Roots

 I stood in the kitchen of my new one bedroom apartment in a panic. What the heck was I supposed to do now? I'd spent my youth baking the occasional batch of cookies, cakes and treats, but never learned how to make a meal like dinner. A Bundt Cake? Sure. A pot roast? Clueless. Now I had to not only cook for myself, but for my new husband as well. I was in serious trouble.

 I thawed out some frozen chicken in the microwave and then broiled the half-rubbery/half-frozen chunks of meat in the oven. When I pulled the pan from the heat, my "meal" was a hardened mess. Tears stung my eyes. My incompetence was acute. Looking at my main course, I realized I had no side dish. Worse, I didn't even know what to make. I opened up a can of green beans and served my first pathetic meal to my new spouse.

 I still remember Matt's face, the look of disappointment etched forever in my mind. I think it was then he realized he had married a child, inexperienced in so many ways.

 He had come from a family with a home-chef mother rivaling Paula Dean in the kitchen where he had become an apt cook under her guidance. A true perfectionist, everything Matt touched turned gold. If he made cookies, they were all exactly the same shape and size—all of them— like they had come from a factory rather than a human hand. If I made cookies, they were all different shapes and sizes and some sank in the middle. My family had been never particular that way. When it came to the kitchen, not only was I uneducated, I really didn't care . . . until now. Suddenly, I understood how malnourished some of my roots were, how unprepared I was to be an adult, let alone a wife. I felt both foolish and ashamed to be so ignorant in an area that was so obviously important, not only to Matt but to a functioning household.

 Being a verbal person, I shared my insecurities with my spouse, but he wasn't much of a talker. Rather than discuss it like a healthy couple with a relationship rooted in communication, we handled our expectations and disappointments on the matter separately. I felt inept and stupid, even rejected by his silence; I could only guess how he felt. His suggestions about my cooking sounded like personal attacks. The frustrated looks he couldn't hide harpooned my heart as I served one pathetic dinner after another.

Those mutually unmet expectations caused a lot of fights. I call them fights because we were both stubborn, opinionated and fiercely independent, pulling out our metaphorical boxing gloves to verbally duke out every misunderstanding. I jabbed because his lack of communication hurt and his suggestions felt like criticisms. He jabbed because, being a perfectionist, he couldn't understand why I couldn't seem to get things right. My ignorance and lack of experience were a constant source of frustration to him. I needed assurance and encouragement from him. He needed precision and results from me. We didn't seem to be able to give these things to one another because we couldn't express them through healthy communication. Our steely armor of pride was too thick.

By our fifth month of marriage, we had a fight of epic proportions. I packed my bags and moved back home with my parents.

Matt never called.

By the fourth day, I was a nervous wreck. I paced the floor. I tried to read a book but couldn't comprehend a single word on the page. Nothing I did quelled the anxious flutters in my stomach. Finally, I called him. I didn't get married to have it fail in the first six months and I certainly wasn't going to let it go without closure.

It was quiet on the other end of the line when I asked, "Why haven't you called me?"

"I decided it was over," he finally said.

I swallowed hard, tears filling my eyes. Not only was I a complete failure at marriage, but I was going to lose the man I loved.

"But now that I hear your voice," he continued, "I think maybe we should give it another try."

I exhaled in relief, grateful for apologies and second chances.

A few hours later, I was squeezing Matt in a grateful vise grip, resolving to be a better wife in every way. This was my marriage and I was determined to make it work.

The Business of Blending

After six months, we left our little apartment behind and moved into a two-bedroom duplex with a two-car garage and small, fenced back yard. We had talked about having a baby, but didn't know when it would happen, even though I had gone off birth control already. By the end of the seventh month of our marriage, I was pregnant.

I was nineteen.

I left my job at the dental office. My employer was downsizing and since I was pregnant I decided not to find a new job. I spent my newly acquired free time visiting my mom and preparing the spare bedroom for our anticipated arrival. Since I had been sewing for ten years, I competently created a complete crib set in bright, bold colors with checkered black and white trim and matching accessories.

During this time, my friend Sally taught me to toll paint.

"You have to load the paint on the corner of the brush after you dip it in water, then stroke like this to blend the color on the wood." She moved her brush effortlessly across the curve of a rose petal to shade part of it. It was beautiful.

I followed her lead, but I either loaded too much paint and too little water on the brush, or too much water and too little paint.

I sighed with frustration.

"You'll get it," Sally said in a patient tone.

I had my doubts.

But I did practice, and eventually I did get it. In fact, I became a rather good painter, completing complex projects.

Matt liked my newly acquired artistic skills and bought a band saw to cut out small ornaments for me so I could paint them for family Christmas gifts. The magazine where I got the ornament designs contained a pattern for a beautiful wooden mantle clock. Matt built the clock from scratch with impeccable craftsmanship. I then painted a detailed picture of a boy and girl waiting anxiously for Santa in a four-poster bed with stockings hanging from the posts and Christmas decorations all around. It turned out to be a lovely cooperative project using both of our talents and we displayed the clock proudly every Christmas from that year on.

I enjoyed these types of projects, and especially Matt's support of them, but he was spending more and more time in his new garage and I often felt lonely. I understood the need for the man-cave, but when the man rarely came out of his cave, and I went to bed alone every night, it got old really fast. Was he recoiling from the pregnant me? Was he overwhelmed with the impending responsibility that a child would bring? Was I a bad wife? Was he still disillusioned with me? I could only guess. He never talked to me about anything. Despite my resolution and attempts to be a better wife, we still couldn't come together communication-wise. We hadn't managed to blend our proverbial brushes to make the right balance between us so that our relationship could blend, flow, and become a thing of beauty. Ironically, though we each had mastered many complex artistic and crafting skills, we could not master the art of communication and the blending of personalities.

One evening, he came in from the garage and grabbed a Popsicle out of the freezer.

Concerned, I asked, "Where's your wedding ring?"

"Oh . . . I must have left it in my toolbox at work." He grabbed his frozen treat and closed the freezer door, adding, "You know I can't wear it when I work or I could lose my finger. Besides, it's just too big. I'm afraid it will fall off."

Never fear, Jen is here! I had the solution.

"We can go get it re-sized," I suggested eagerly.

He mumbled something in agreement and went back outside. My gut feared something was wrong. I hardly dared guess what, but at least he had agreed to my suggestion.

A wedding ring is a symbol of commitment, and not wearing it meant that commitment had waned for some reason. My heart broke a little that night.

A few weeks later, I almost skipped into the house as Matt wore his newly-sized wedding ring home from the jeweler. Surely he would wear it all the time now!

But no, he didn't.

"It's too tight now," he said, "and too hard to get on and off easily at work."

It ended up in a box of "special things" tucked out of sight in a dresser drawer.

We were separating; I could feel it. And I hated it. I wanted so badly for us to blend, like that paint and water on the brush. I reminded myself that those skills took time to learn. I clung to the hope that in time, we would be able to blend as a couple.

Little Rejections

I put our one-year-old, Kale, down for the night, sighing with exhaustion. He looked so peaceful sleeping there in his crib. It had been a long year, adjusting to being a new mother, and I had learned quickly that I would not have much help from Matt. I slipped out of Kale's room and headed toward the family room where Matt was watching television. Tired and lonely, I was desperate to feel his arms around me. He always seemed to be either working late or in the garage and I missed him.

I sat down next to him but he was too engrossed in his program to notice me. Taking a different approach, I placed a pillow on his lap and laid my head down on it. He moved his hands out of the way to accommodate the pillow, resting them at his sides on the couch. I lay there, waiting to see if he would touch me. Maybe put his hands on my shoulders, arms, back, anything, but no.

He wouldn't touch me.

As the minutes ticked by, my heart grew heavier and heavier. Why wouldn't he hold me? Did he even love me anymore? I felt so alone.

After a short time, I quietly got up and walked to my dark bedroom where I collapsed on the bed, stifling the tears in my pillow.

Settling In

Several years passed. We added a daughter, Chelsey, to our family and purchased our first home in a quiet neighborhood in a town about 15 minutes from downtown Sacramento. In this cute yellow house with white trim, I started to feel grounded for the first time. We bought furniture and began building a home. I stocked the kitchen cupboards with necessities and hand-painted a sunflower chair border around the dining nook. I painted the walls in every room with color, and sewed curtains and pillows and bedding to coordinate with the walls and décor for each room.

Matt poured an aggregate patio and built a beautiful redwood sunshade out back, his workmanship flawless. He poured mowing strips, put in a lawn, built a shed and designed planter and gardening beds that I filled with plants, flowers and vegetables.

I stayed home to raise our two beautiful children. We spent our days at the park or splashing on the slippery slide in our sun-filled California back yard. We made art projects and read together, played together, laughed together. My kids were my joy, a gift that washed away my loneliness.

With this shared love of our children, Matt and I were able to create some fun family memories, like trips to Disneyland and extravagant Christmases. Our children seemed to bond us together in some ways. Through them, I felt connected to him again, and any loneliness I did feel was consumed in the creative acts of painting, sewing and new hobbies like floral design and reading.

I began writing music again, a hobby I had started at age fifteen, and had continued to pursue sporadically over the years. My grandmother was instrumental in this pursuit. She had passed away and left each of her grandchildren some money. With mine, I bought a full-sized digital keyboard with weighted keys to replace the small portable Casio keyboard I'd been trying to write on. As songwriting began to play a largely therapeutic role in my life, the keyboard was a great blessing. These pleasant, productive and healthy ways to cope with any loneliness I felt in my relationship were good. It was a peaceful time, lacking, but peaceful. I could deal with that.

The List of Devastation

It was about 5:30 in the afternoon as I sat on the floral print couch reading a book and watching Kale and Chelsey play Lego on the floor. The sun was lowering in the sky, its orange-colored rays peeking through the horizontal blinds on the west-facing window of the family room. My nearly two-year-old daughter climbed up in her miniature recliner and laid her head on the padded arm, sucking her thumb, blanket in hand, as Matt walked through the front door.

He bent down. "Can I have a hug?" He asked her.

She shook her blond head back and forth as she closed her eyes, obviously too tired to acquiesce his request.

"How about you, Kiddo?" He asked Kale as he stretched out his arms, "How about a hug for your dad?"

"No," was the reply from Kale as he busily assembled his Lego creation. "I'm playing."

"I'll give you one," I said eagerly as I rose from the couch.

Matt looked at me, straightened his spine, dropped his arms to his side and walked out of the room.

Rejection lodged in my throat and refused to let me swallow. I know he'd heard me because he'd looked straight at me. He deliberately chose to ignore me and silently refused my gesture of affection. Why? What was going on?!

Preparing dinner was a blur of anxiety, a whirlwind of thoughts, questions and fears. How would he be when he came in from the garage to eat dinner? Would he ignore me again? Be indifferent to me?

I didn't find out; he didn't come inside to eat dinner with us.

I laid in my bed in the dark of night waiting for him to come inside. The clock moved at a slug's pace, but he finally came to bed.

"What is going on with you?" I calmly asked. "You seem like you don't want anything to do with me."

He was quiet for a long time . . .

An hour later, the bed was covered with piles of Kleenex, proof that my eyes and nose were flowing like Niagara Falls. It was the way he said it that sent every painful emotion in my body rushing together and bursting out my eyes in sheets of tears. My stomach churned and my body trembled as his words invaded my ears, thumped against my skull and devastated my heart.

I don't love you anymore. I'm not attracted to you. I can't figure out why I even married you in the first place, you're not like any of the girls I dated. They were all skinny and five foot four or smaller with green or blue eyes. You just look old for your age. And when you cry your nose gets red and looks even bigger. You could really use plastic surgery . . .

The world as I knew it stopped spinning. The room expanded and contracted around me, squeezing the breath from my lungs. Every bit of security I had felt up to that moment crumbled to dust. My husband hated me. The person who was supposed to love me the most was, in fact, telling me he didn't love me at all.

Not only did he not love me, he didn't like anything about me. I was a mistake, a bad decision, an unfit and unworthy selection of a wife next to the beautiful ghosts of his past.

My life had instantly become the ruins of Pompeii. I was demolished.

This decimation hadn't come during an explosive argument where two people say things they don't mean and then make up with apologies. Rather, it came during a calm conversation, stealthy and destructive to my tender heart. No apologies or regrets ever came. No healing balm soothed my wounds. I was forever and irreversibly changed in an excruciating and deforming way.

After that night, I began to wake from my sleep often with heart palpitations and a horrific feeling, like impending death. This continued for so long that I finally went to the doctor, insisting that he monitor my heart. After all, it had been broken. He insisted it was just stress. The doctor was right.

Matt didn't say he wanted a divorce, just that he was supremely unhappy with me. And I was supposed to live with that? I didn't know how. We had two small children and I wanted to keep my family together more than anything. I had never been a quitter and didn't want to start now. So I decided to do the only thing I thought would save our marriage.

Become perfect.

Funny, how I suddenly forgot what an impossibility that is, becoming perfect. Though I was already very fit physically, I started working out even more. I kept the house as immaculate as possible and tried to be the very best cook I could, even though I had improved leaps and bounds since those first few years. I placed impossible standards on myself and whenever I fell short of them, or what I believed Matt wanted me to be, I apologized. Many times he didn't even have to say a word; I would apologize before he had the chance to express his disapproval. If I could "beat him to the punch," it was less painful. But overcompensation and reaching for impossible standards are oppressive taskmasters. I began to lose myself, wishing to be anything but myself, so that my husband would love me and approve of me.

Soon after that, Matt made two big decisions that would forever alter the course of our lives. One, he stopped going to church, which had been one of the only things we still shared in common. Two, he made a personal decision that had huge consequences for our family that ultimately led to us moving out of state.

Life was changing, and I didn't like the direction it was headed.

Changes

    I leaned on a large cardboard box in my family room as I watched the terror play and replay on the television screen. The twin towers had been destroyed and the nation was devastated. How symbolic.

    After a catastrophe, there is often an evaluation of priorities about what's important. People come together in ways they hadn't been able to before. As the country was going through its healing process after the terrorist attacks, Matt and I were undergoing a shift as well. Only ours wasn't a healing shift. We thought it was, but it was merely an escape of sorts. We were running from a past we didn't know how to fix, hoping that new geography, new employment and new people would heal what was internally dysfunctional.

    I looked around the family room at the piles of moving boxes and wondered if our house sale would still close in ten days in light of the national crisis. Would I put these boxes in a truck soon? Or would I be unpacking them and staying?

    Fortunately, and unfortunately, we moved September 21st as planned. With tears in my eyes, we drove east toward Utah—a state where I never wanted to live, much less raise my children. I said my final goodbyes to my family support system (my parents who lived close by), and wondered what it would be like living in a state with a husband who didn't love me and where I didn't have any close family members or friends to lean on. I watched the city lights fade behind me as we entered the dark freeway and tried to remain hopeful, even as trepidation wrapped its cold fingers around my heart.

Contention Rising

"Here Aunt Jeni," my darling, three-year-old niece Mandy said as she handed me a picture she had scribbled with crayons.

"Thanks sweetie, that's so pretty." I rose from the couch and walked toward the kitchen holding her hand. "Let's put it on the refrigerator."

She nodded with a smile of approval then ran off to play with her cousins, whom she rarely saw as she lived on the East Coast.

My younger sister was in town and I was babysitting for the evening while she and her husband attended the theater with friends.

Matt was in the garage, as usual, and in an especially irritable mood. His job had become incredibly stressful. It had always been commission-based, and in California the economy supported those commissions (and our bank account) amply. But in Utah, a different culture neglected to provide the necessary opportunity to acquire a sufficient income for our standard of living. On edge, he snapped easily and often. Tonight was no exception.

We ended up screaming at each other over something stupid until I could no longer stand it. Our immature actions were upsetting the kids. Desperate for some peace, I needed to get out of the house.

"I'm leaving," I announced as I headed to the bedroom.

"Oh no, you're not," he shouted authoritatively.

I promptly began packing a bag for the night. No one was going to tell me what to do! I gathered the kids and their things and we headed out to the car. I turned the key, but nothing happened.

Sheer rage shot through my body, my blood pressure rising in anger as I realized why the car wouldn't start. "How dare he do this to me again!"

I ran into the house, "Hook the car back up," I insisted. "You can't keep me here!"

He shook his head side to side with a smug look of victory.

"You have no right to control me! If I want to leave I should be able to!"

He refused to oblige me.

Being stubborn and unwilling to submit to being controlled I did the only thing I could think of. I called the only family we had around . . . his parents.

Within 30 minutes his father came to pick me up. He didn't say a word the entire drive to his house. I knew he was uncomfortable; I was uncomfortable. I didn't want to bring him into this, but I couldn't let Matt have yet another victory of control. Dignity deserves to hold her head high now and again, and tonight I was claiming mine.

I put the kids down for the night in the spare bedroom of my in-laws basement and, at length, fell asleep wondering how long I could stand to suffer in the prison of a bad relationship.

Desert Bloom

A tear rolled down my cheek as I held the homemade card in my hands. It was made out of bright orange card stock. On the front there was a flower in a pot crafted from construction paper and Spanish moss. Written inside the card were the words:

Bloom where you are planted.

"Thanks, Mom, but I hate it here," I said aloud to myself.

It had been two years since the move and things had continued to be terribly challenging. I had no family that I was close with, or friends—at least not the kind I could tell my most personal problems to. I talked to mom on the phone a lot, sometimes daily, but missed the comfort of physical support that my extended family had given me through the years.

I stared at the card, the words blurring as my eyes filled with tears. My loneliness was punctuated by the silence as Kale and Chelsey played quietly in the basement of our rambler-style home.

"I don't know how to bloom here," I whispered.

I felt horribly wilted inside. Would I ever thrive in my barren environment?

I placed the card on my dresser where I would be reminded of the possibility it expressed, even though that possibility felt entirely out of my reach.

A Seed Planted

I had the window rolled down on my Honda Accord as the April sunshine poured onto my dash, warming my hands as they rested on the steering wheel. I was driving through town, making my weekly shopping trip when I saw a sign that advertised the Miss Riverton Scholarship Pageant. I made a mental note of the date and time. *What a fun mother-daughter date that would be!*

The night came and my then seven-year-old daughter and I went to the pageant. I had never been to a pageant before. I found the live pageant to be a very different experience from the few I'd seen on television. The girls all looked . . . normal. Of course, they were all talented, accomplished and beautiful but definitely not perfect, like the girls appeared on T.V. I found that very refreshing.

Chelsey and I had a great time, went home and all was well. But in the days that followed, an incessant feeling kept telling me that I should do a pageant.

What?! Me? No way! I argued with the thought. *They probably don't even have pageants for married women!*

Over the next few days, this impression nagged at me until I finally went Online to research the possibility.

Pageants for married women DO exist!

I wrestled with what this could mean for me. I was compelled to find out more and yet, repulsed by my own insanity at considering such a foolish idea. Still, I ended up doing more research and ordered a book on pageants from the library.

The book came in and I picked it up. I sprawled back on the floral print of the living room couch to read this "book of secrets." I skimmed through most of it, stopping on random pages. Vaseline on the teeth, glue on the butt, choosing the perfect swimsuit . . .

Swimsuit?!!!

I chucked the book across the room. It landed with a thud in the library basket, where it belonged.

Yeah, right. Definitely NOT for me!

World Upside Down

My mind was reeling as I heard the words.

"I want a divorce," Matt said with deep sincerity.

I steadied myself by sitting down on the couch. It felt like one of those scenes in a movie where the person speaks the "incomprehensible words" and the character's world suddenly starts to spin and everything gets fuzzy and they can't hear.

When the sensation finally passed and I understood what he was saying, my heart began to race with panic. What was I going to do? I had no education. Many times throughout our marriage I had brought up the subject of pursuing my degree, but he always found a reason to postpone it or to brush it aside by defining it as "unnecessary for a housewife." I also hadn't worked outside the home in almost a decade. Now I was in a state with no family around me, completely isolated. Where would I go?

It was as if someone had just decreed a death sentence on my future. How would I take care of myself? What would happen to my children? My stomach churned. I wrapped my arms around my torso, the sensation of vomit climbing up my esophagus.

The entire year had been hellish. January had started with the death of my dear grandmother which was followed by escalating arguments between me and Matt. His emotional withdrawals had reached an all-time high and I felt more rejected than ever. His job had become unbearable for him and money was getting tight. We decided to put our big, new, beautiful home up for sale and sold our new car as well. In September, he finally quit his job. Two weeks later, I found out I was pregnant. In shock and awe, we wondered how we would be able to parent a child amidst so much chaos. In addition, we had given away all of our baby stuff before moving. As far as we had been concerned, our childbearing days were over.

Apparently not.

It took a few weeks to get used to the idea, but we started to get excited about the thought of having another baby. It had bonded us as a couple before, perhaps it would again.

Kale and Chelsey were especially excited about the news. But as misfortune would have it, I miscarried a few months later.

Like everything that year, we dealt with the disappointment the best we could. But the challenges kept coming, one after another, like drops of rain in a relentless storm. Before we had time to barely grasp the meaning of one challenge, another plopped on our heads, leaving us reeling.

Still grieving over the loss of the pregnancy, we received a notice in the mail from our mortgage company stating that they'd messed up the charges on our escrow account and that we owed back taxes on our property. Consequently, our house payment increased three hundred dollars per month for the next three months. We were unemployed and it was just before Christmas.

The New Year brought a massive rainstorm that flooded our basement, damage we had to repair to be able to sell the house. So much loss, stress and strain built like a volcano and our relationship was about to blow up. There were times I couldn't even cry I was so numb.

And now this decree! My head was still spinning from Matt's declaration of divorce and, being in a state of distress, I called my Bishop for counsel. A few hours later, this kind and gentle man sat on the chair across from me. Because the Bishop had asked to see us together, Matt reluctantly sat on the couch by himself.

"Seek first to understand others before seeking to be understood," he said as he counseled us in how to save our relationship. "And I would advise you to not to make a decision until you both agree on the same course of action."

Miraculously, Matt took his words to heart. We stayed together, clinging to shredded hope.

In March our house finally sold and we moved in with my in-laws. This would give Matt time to make a fresh start and find a new career. We hoped the change would save our relationship. Matt firmly believed that if he could just be happy in his job, he could be happy at home. I was willing to support his need for a career change. I wanted him to be happy. Maybe then we could have a chance. So we packed up our stuff yet again, putting much of it in storage, and moved into his parents' basement. Everything had already fallen apart and turned upside down. How could things get any worse?

Book II

This is Healing?

"Sometimes a breakdown can be the beginning of a kind of breakthrough, a way of living in advance through a trauma that prepares you for a future of radical transformation."
~Cherrie Moraga

Soul Cleaning

It's been a lousy afternoon. I've really been struggling lately. Nothing is changing for Matt and me. He doesn't seem to have the energy or drive to pursue a whole new career. Though he got a job, it's worse than the last one, and basically in the same industry. He's working 12-hour graveyard shifts and the kids and I have to act like ghosts during the day so he can sleep. It's hard to keep quiet all day long when you're homeschooling two children.

To say I feel stressed is an understatement. I feel like we are in limbo, stagnant. I've given up my beautiful home, all my nice things, my personal space and my hobbies so that we could better our situation. I keep giving up more and more of myself to accommodate a relationship that never changes.

I'm frustrated, to say the least.

A knock sounds at my front door. It's my friend Tami. I haven't known her very long, but she wants to know how I am doing. Until now I have never told her my troubles, but as soon as I open my mouth, I begin crying and pouring out my pathetic excuse for a life on her unsuspecting ears.

"You need to ground, shield and detach," she says with the calm and wisdom of a yogi as she sits down on the couch across from me.

I wrinkle my brow in confusion, "Huh?"

"Grounding is connecting to the earth in some way, either through meditation or spending time in nature. It can even be done while consciously doing mundane chores like cleaning or weed pulling, but grounding always connects you to your Source, your foundation."

I absorb her words for a minute. "I read daily from my core religious text and pray. Am I not already grounding?" I ask.

"It's not enough to pray and read," she says. "You must be mentally still and connect with your foundation through nature, meditation, or visualization. You must also shield yourself from the negative energy that surrounds you, and detach from your emotions."

I swallow hard. That sounds like a lot. "How do I do that?"

She suggests that I visualize a bubble around myself that only positive energy can pass through, and that I picture everything else just bouncing off of that bubble. "You choose what you will let into your energy field."

"Is this possible?"

"Yes, with practice," she says as she nods. "Detaching from your emotions is simply a habit of observing your feelings rather than engaging in them habitually."

I listen intently. I am desperate and willing to consider anything, no matter how strange it may sound to me.

"Pray for your own individual vision of potential," she continues, "to be guided to those teachers who can help you with your individual curriculum for healing."

Curriculum for healing? I feel slightly bewildered by her gush of instruction, but they say that when the student is ready, the teacher appears. In moments like these, when I'm about to give up, I've discovered those are the times I need to hold hope even tighter because, when I do, there is always a light around the bend. This time that light has come in the form of a new friend offering new tools I've never tried before. Could her suggestions really work? Could they be the answers I need?

I wrap my arms around her in a grateful hug.

"After you claw your way through the darkness," she says as she passes through the threshold of my front door, "then, and only then, can God use you for greater purposes." She smiles. "Keep cleaning house."

I close the door behind her and exhale deeply.

Sitting with the Enemy

Tami stopped by again and dropped off a book for me to read called *I Know I'm in There Somewhere* by Helen G. Brenner, Ph.D. After reading it, I realize I've become distrustful of my own feelings and experiences. Life, and years of criticism, have taught me that my judgments and perceptions are wrong. I have shut down much of my intuition and ignored much of my emotional experience, except for the painful experiences I cannot ignore. What would it be like to trust myself? To feel confident enough to make decisions and not worry that they are the wrong decisions? To not second guess myself all the time? I don't even know.

I pause in my reading to write for a minute. I need to try the process of *sitting with my feelings*, as the author suggests. I take my extremely tense body to sit in the tub. I close my eyes and try to relax. I concentrate on how I am feeling physically. I am tense in my shoulders and up my neck and head. I feel pressure on my chest and my eye is twitching. I focus on some of the issues that I think might be contributing to the physical feelings I am experiencing: wanting to buy a home, finances, feeling spread too thin, and being overwhelmed with life and my relationship with Matt. I take each one individually and just feel the feelings associated with each issue.

Fear rises at the thought of buying a home, and I realize this is based on past experiences. But I also feel it a necessary risk we need to take that will allow me to "root" myself again.

Finances are connected to all my stresses and feelings. I sift through some possible causes but they don't *feel* deep enough. I search deeper and suddenly have an epiphany. In my mind's eye, I see myself in a tiny little room surrounded by darkness on the outside. It feels so confining. There is so much pressure. The amazing and profound thing I discover is that the greatest pressure is on the inside of the room. I am putting all this pressure on myself from the inside!!! I open my eyes in surprise. I can see how I am blocking out things that need to get in and how I am also blocking my own self-expression, direction and potential!

I close my eyes again and the tiny space appears in my mind. This process is much like dream imagery or spontaneous visualization, but this time I actually have a key around my neck. It is a long old-fashioned key. When I put it in the key hole and open the door a crack, air gushes in. I actually physically catch my breath and open my eyes, sitting up in the tub.

I exhale, re-close my eyes and lean back against the warm porcelain. Again I am brought to this room in my mind. It begins expanding. With each breath I take, the room grows larger and larger. Suddenly, there are pink, blue, purple and yellow flowers everywhere; buds and green growth cover everything. I notice a window in the room that wasn't there before, revealing a bright and sunny outside. I open the window and more air rushes in. Physically, I feel an intense need to get outside and breathe the fresh air! With my muscles more relaxed, I feel lighter. How liberating! Is this what it's like to listen to your feelings?

It wasn't scary or painful like I thought it might be. My emotions are not the enemy after all! They are simply an energy that provides communication, experience and knowledge to my mind in a form other than words.

What have I been so afraid of all these years?

Bedroom Woes

I lift myself up and down in a repetitive motion as I do push-ups on my bedroom floor. With every repetition, I notice bits of paper, crushed Goldfish cracker crumbs and broken pieces of pencil lead in the carpet. This room doesn't get vacuumed anywhere near as often as the rest of the house.

I sit up and look at my unmade bed. I never make my bed anymore. When did this happen? I used to always keep a clean and organized bedroom. I suppose it doesn't help that I'm living in my in-laws' basement. In addition to a five-piece bedroom set, the room also holds: a large recliner, a drafting table, my full-size keyboard, a treadmill and a bunch of other junk that should go somewhere else but can't because of space constraints.

Over the last few years, we have been through some very difficult trials. Challenges have created a smaller world for us in so many ways. I find it significant that our physical surroundings have contracted as well.

Another revealing parallel is that I never open the drapes in this room. Like my heart, I keep my bedroom dark.

I haven't really noticed the state of this room until now. Probably because I just close the door and rarely come in here. Actually, I avoid my room as much as possible. I hate the clutter and mess. The outside rooms that people might see get cleaned and vacuumed regularly, but not this room.

Matt never complains about the mess in here, but if there is mess in any other part of the house, he complains like crazy. He can't stand it! Is this simply conditioning? I don't think so. The more I learn about the physical, spiritual, emotional and mental connections of the body, the more I see correlations and parallels to those things in every aspect of my life.

In dream interpretation, the bedroom represents the most intimate part of the soul. If our bedroom—our most personal, intimate physical space—is a reflection of the condition of our inner lives, then it makes sense why we would both be able to tolerate the outward clutter of our bedroom. We are both emotional wrecks. Likewise, we keep the parts of the house that other people can see well groomed, just as we do our external countenances. We wear masks. Our home mimics our emotional states and tolerances.

As I continue to de-clutter my soul, I must pay attention to my personal, physical space as an indicator of my emotional state. If my bedroom mimics the state of my heart, perhaps it's time to get it organized, let some light into it daily, and spend a little more time in it.

An Unusual Drug

Healing is hard work. I don't like all the junk that's surfacing, lots of raw and ugly emotions. I already hate what I look like and how I feel. To discover so many unpleasant faults within me leaves me feeling pathetic and lame much of the time.

I was reading a minute ago and my head began to feel fuzzy, crowded and weird. I stopped reading and grabbed my journal and pen. Lately, I have been reading every spare second I can find. I'm reading a diverse amount of subject matter and nothing is really tying together for me. Why am I reading so much?

As I reflect, I understand what is going on. I am filling my head with so much information that I can't hear my own thoughts. That way, I don't have to feel all these crappy emotions. I don't really know what to do with the information that's coming into my awareness about what I need to change in order to be whole. I am still trying to figure all this out. Reading distracts me in a "healthy" way.

I suppose reading has become my drug of choice, my addiction. We all have them. Many of them masquerade as healthy hobbies, but anything that is used to excess, or as a coping tool can become an addiction, a drug of sorts.

The more I think about addictions, the more I understand that even thoughts and beliefs can be addictions. Feeding the ego can be an addiction. Fear is an addiction. Addictions help to maintain equilibrium in our lives. We want familiar feelings. We want good feelings. Addictions help us feel comfortable, good, and normal.

I am no expert on addictions but this makes sense to me. I am at a point where my equilibrium is constantly being knocked out of whack because I am constantly questioning and evaluating my life while trying to heal. So many issues keep surfacing in the healing process that I hardly know what to do with them. So I grasp in every direction for something familiar, something to keep me feeling even and safe. I read. I feel safe in the pool of other people's words and thoughts. I can open or close the book on those thoughts at any time. It is a safe drug. I can take as much as I want and justify my "drug use" with words like *knowledge* and *education*. But I know it's really just a distraction and a coping tool. I had no idea that reading so much could actually lead to physical feelings of fuzzy-headedness and kind of a disconnect from life. I guess every drug, even the safe ones, have physical consequences in one form or another.

Permission to Pretend

This is crazy. I can't possibly audition for a part in the community theater! This particular theater organization has won awards. And I'm certainly no actress!

The sign said auditions are tomorrow. Can I really be prepared by tomorrow? I have driven down main street hundreds of times and never even noticed those audition signs. Why today? I swallow hard as I consider the fact that if I do go to the audition, I will likely make a fool out of myself. Still, I cannot deny the inner knowing drive that is telling me I *need* to do this.

I close the door to the den and begin singing, "On my own . . . pretending he's beside me." It will have to do. I know this song and I don't really have time to be picky.

The next morning, I am sitting at the local junior high school with a bunch of strangers. Feeling completely out of my element with the theater buffs and singers who are excited to be there, I rack my brain for the reason I felt I needed to do this but nothing surfaces. I don't feel nervous as I am led into a room to learn 16 bars of a piece from the production. My expectations for success aren't that high and I'm quite certain I won't get a part.

Next comes dancing. I love to dance! I make a new friend, Kristie. We laugh and dance and I have a blast as my body slips easily into the memory of moving to music just like when I was a teenager. The directors come into the stuffy room where we have been dancing for nearly an hour. They watch us; take some notes and then exit.

Next, we are led to the stage to do cold readings. I have never done a cold reading. My stomach skips with nerves as I take my place on the stage and try to vocally act out what I am reading. I know I stink; I have never been able to fake emotion.

We are then ushered into the auditorium, five at a time, to sing the female solo part we learned earlier. We stand in a row in front of the directors, each woman taking her turn to sing the 16 bars. I do the best I can, and feel okay about my performance, but there are much better singers in this group.

We return to the stage to sing solos. I have always been a nervous and physically inexpressive singer; I'm boring to watch. In this setting, I know I need to step it up and gesture while I'm singing. This is hard for me. Waves of foolishness wash over me as I walk to the center of the stage with a forced smile on my face. I know full well the power of movement while performing because I've taught it to others. I just have trouble doing it myself. I exhale stealthily to calm myself, and as the music begins, I suddenly decide I have nothing to lose. I gesture and surprise! It feels natural and amazing! The movement actually creates a pathway for all my nervous energy to flow through!

As I finish the song, one of the directors says, "Forget Annie, let's do *Les Miserables*." He's smiling, "Good job."

A genuine smile breaks across my face in return for his as I take the compliment. It seems a small victory, but for me, it is a huge breakthrough. I risked and was rewarded with a sense of satisfaction, achievement and growth.

A week later, I stand outside City Hall with a dropped jaw. I have not only been given a part in the production, I have been cast as the lead love interest to Oliver Warbucks in *Annie Warbucks: The Sequel to Annie*.

What the heck am I going to do now?!

I turn slowly on my heel and walk back to my car in a daze, knowing that I will have to break through even greater blocks and fears in the next 12 weeks to pull this off. I hope I don't disappoint everybody and ruin the whole production.

Breaking through Walls

"I'm not convinced," the director says. "You need to look deep into his eyes and tell him you love him."

I stand frozen. 25 people are all staring at me, waiting.

"This is the wedding scene!"

I can feel her frustration with me, but I don't know how to do this. I don't know *how* to *act* like I love someone. I've never been able to fake that!

"Again," she says.

We run the scene again, but I freeze up and feel my phoniness as I come to those dreaded lines.

An exasperated sigh passes through her lips. "Let's take a break for five."

My shoulders slump in discouragement as the director's husband, Josh, pulls me aside. A seasoned actor and former rock and roll band member, he knows something about performing. This isn't the first time he has taken me aside and told me that I need to give more in my acting. Tonight, he gives me a crash mentoring course on performance.

"On stage you have to be larger than life," he says. "You have to step into the character's shoes and become that person. *You have to let go and not worry about what other people think.* The dumber you feel, the better the job you are doing."

I know he's right but I am scared of looking foolish. I already feel like such an idiot and failure most of the time in my personal life. Do I really need to have that fact recognized publicly?

"Keep working at it." He pats me on the shoulder. "The director wouldn't have given you the part if she didn't think you could do it." He smiles.

I feel doubt as I drag my feet back toward my mark on the floor. We run the scene again. I can either give up, defeated, or I can really try and tackle this fear.

I sigh.

When the time comes, I force myself to say my lines with meaning. It feels like I am pushing through a thick concrete wall of emotion. I can feel my face burning with heat as the entire room stares at me expressing this fake but convincing "love" for my co-star.

"That's it!" The director squeals with delight. "*Much* better! That's a wrap on the scene." She claps her hands loudly.

I am sweating. I rush to the door and push my face into the cool evening breeze, letting it blow the redness away. I am so embarrassed.

A few hours later, I lie in my bed and run through the events of the day. Why had it been so hard for me to play that scene? Why had it felt like pulling teeth? I'm afraid of judgment for sure, but it feels like there is more going on under the surface than just that.

Epiphany!

I am vulnerable. To allow feelings of love to surface and direct them toward another man, even if it's just acting, terrifies me. To pretend an expression of love authentic enough for the audience to buy scares me to death. I think I'm afraid I might really fall in love! My life is so void of male attention and approval, it's pathetic. I fear I am weak. Am I blocking my acting success because of fear of weakness? Fear that I don't know my own strength? Fear that I will violate my own integrity?

The weeks pass, and as I become more at ease with emotional expression through acting, I discover something amazing! I *haven't* fallen in love with my co-star! My fears were completely irrational!

Fears are simply that, fears. Not truth. Yes, I am vulnerable and my needs are not being met, but I am not desperate or unfaithful. I love Matt and my integrity is sound.

Opening night comes and we run our show through the week. Saturday brings a double performance, one matinée and one evening show. I wake up that morning with a painfully swollen throat, so swollen I can barely speak. There are no understudies for my role.

I head to the instant care clinic where I get a mega-shot of antibiotic, but I'm told I won't see any improvement for at least 12 hours and curtain is in three.

During the performances, I shiver in the wings with a full-blown fever. Every second that I am not performing, I sleep on the dressing room floor. I don't even care that the floor is hard, dirty and I have no pillow or blanket.

My solo is a huge concern. I haven't even tried to sing yet and it's approaching fast. I step out onto the stage, the scenes passing like lightning. The orchestra suddenly starts playing the introduction to my song, my cue to step toward the white gazebo that is part of the set.

"God help me," is my silent prayer, the same one I have been uttering all day. "Please let me sing when I open my mouth."

Miracles always seem to occur for other people, but tonight I experience one for myself. I sing my entire song without any difficulty at all. After the last note, the lights fade and I walk off stage shaking from head to toe with illness. The crowd is whistling, screaming and cheering. They have no idea I am sick.

I collapse into a chair backstage, partly from exhaustion, partly in gratitude for the blessing of faith that knocks down the walls between Heaven and Earth by delivering small miracles, even to people like me.

Another Haunting Thought

I am entering the grocery store and spot one of my community theater co-stars in line at the checkout stand. I haven't seen her for months!

"You look fabulous Cindy," I say.

"Thanks," she says with a smile. "I am competing for Mrs. Utah in a few weeks."

"I'd love to come support you," I say with excitement. "Where is it being held?"

After getting the event details from her we part ways. I buy the tickets Online and take my daughter to the event.

Sitting in the audience, I watch a stage full of lovely and accomplished women glide across the floor in their gowns when an uncomfortable feeling rises from my gut to my mind. *"You should do a pageant,"* the little voice inside me prompts. I haven't had that thought in three years! My soul is taunting me again. What is it with this pageant stuff?!

After the winner is announced, we make our way to the stage to congratulate my friend on her efforts.

I get a close-up view of the winner and some of the other women. They are gorgeous! *I could never do this!*

Chelsey and I head home, and life is pretty much normal, except for the annoying, recurring feeling that a pageant is in my imminent future.

I pass through the weeks, struggling with my heart and finally submit to the annoying thought.

"Okay," I say aloud to myself. "I'll compete in three years from now. Heaven knows it's gonna take me that long to even be remotely prepared!"

I grab a pen and paper and start writing a list of the things I need to do, become and accomplish to feel worthy to compete: Speak a foreign language, earn my bachelor's degree, actively participate in community service regularly, make my own money so I can pay for it all. I continue writing . . . for three pages. The requirements get more and more complex and harder and harder to reach.

I tuck the paper in my "goals" binder—the binder that has become a graveyard of sorts, holding the corpses of unfulfilled dreams that have never been more than a scrawl on the page. I already feel defeated and I haven't even begun to prepare.

As the months pass I begin feeling more and more emotional and physical tension. How can I compete in a pageant? I am ugly and unaccomplished. Not to mention, in this pageant the husbands escort their wives on stage during the evening gown part of the competition. There's *no way* Matt will escort me on stage! I don't think he even likes me anymore. We never talk; we're just two strangers under the same roof.

October arrives and my resolve weakens even more, much like the faded and fragile fall leaves outside. I attend an event for the women in my church. We have a lovely dinner followed by a guest speaker, none other than the current Miss Utah.

Good grief!

Her words are inspirational and deliver a personal message right to my heart. "You don't have to win a beauty pageant to fulfill your life mission," she says.

A huge sigh escapes my lungs and tension melts from my shoulders as I release myself from a commitment I don't really want to pursue. Why do I get myself into emotional agreements that twist me all up inside and then wait for "messages" from outside sources to give me "permission" to absolve myself from those agreements? Why can't I just be detached and sensible? Only take on those things that are realistic and don't cause me undue stress? Will I ever learn?

I go home and tear up my impossible goal sheet into a hundred pieces, a joyous release from unrealistic expectations and a situation that probably would humiliate me. I am in no position to be competing in a pageant!

The Pit of Hell

"Please God . . . please help me!"

I am on my knees by the floral couch in the den, the door closed. "I can't do this anymore." The tears stream down my cheeks. I struggle to breathe. My chest feels like it's in a vise grip.

"I . . . hate . . . myself." The words come out as a broken whisper, my sobs punctuating what my voice can't convey. I bury my head in the cushions, letting the fabric absorb the water dripping from my eyes and nose. "I hate myself," I say with more conviction. "Please God, I am begging you. I hate who I've become. My own husband doesn't even love me. I don't love me." I gasp for breath and cry some more, fearing I won't be able to stop.

The words of my friend Tami, in whom I confided a few months earlier, throb through my brain with a recurring stab, "Maybe you're just entering the darkness now and you'll have to claw your way out."

More tears.

If I am just entering the darkness now then what have the last 12 years been?! I grab at my chest, certain I will die from emotional overload.

They say that when you hit the bottom of the barrel, there is no place left to go but up. I am at the bottom of my barrel, but I don't know *how* to get up, and it is so dark . . . so very dark. All I can do is languish here, like some lame animal that needs to be put out of its misery.

"How do I get out of this? Please, God? Where are you?"

Time lapses through bursts of crying and pleading, begging and groveling that God will somehow save me from myself. But nothing happens. No answers come.

How can I survive feeling this way? I can't do it!

Whether by the mercy of God, or simply dried up tear ducts, I finally stop crying and collapse in an emotional heap on the floor. What had Tami said? That I would have to claw my way through the darkness? That I was metaphorically hanging from a cliff and would need to pull myself back up?

Why me? Why can't God save me? Why can't he pull me out of this mess? I don't have the strength to fight anymore. I just want the feelings to go away!

I lay like a limp noodle on the floor, time indeterminable, exhausted.

The front door suddenly makes its familiar creak. The kids are done playing outside. I rush to the bathroom, fix my mascara-stained face and go out to the kitchen to fix dinner.

Attempt at Easy

Change doesn't usually happen quickly. Even with intermittent epiphanies, tension mounts when you feel you can't change things. Desperation is an enemy to good sense, but can masquerade as sensibility.

"I'm going to get plastic surgery," I announce to Matt, who looks a little surprised. But surprise soon gives way to a smile of approval.

"Well, it's the perfect time, we have the money," he says, eyes bright.

I am annoyed by his support. Why can't he just tell me he loves me the way I am? Why does he have to agree that I'll look better and be happier with a changed face? Doesn't he know how conflicted I am over all this?!

In the following days, he helps me research doctors. We find one who does fabulous work, has great credentials and who is well-known for his exemplary skills. The consultation reveals potential results that are quite astounding. I am beautiful, at least in the computer manipulated images.

Still, I wrestle deeply with the decision. Part of me wants this surgery more than anything, and believes it is the only way to ever feel peace within myself and my marriage. Another part of me knows that it's a desperate attempt to win Matt's affection and escape feeling ugly. Part of me wants to rebel from appeasing him, and another part of me knows that my problems are more than skin deep and will not resolve just because I have surgery. I am so confused.

Several weeks pass. I call a few more doctors and set up a few more consultations, but I don't feel motivated to go to any of them.

"I hit another deer," Matt yells with exasperation as he walks in the door from work one spring evening. "We're getting the hell out of Alpine."

I am surprised by his declaration. Part of me wondered if we would ever move from his parent's basement. Within three short weeks, we make an offer on a home. The money for my surgery is instantly gone. The decision has been made for me. I will not be getting plastic surgery after all.

A sense of relief washes over me, followed by a wave of panic. What will I do now? How will I ever be whole? Will I ever feel beautiful? Will Matt ever love me?

Alone in my room I look up. "How could you do this to me God?" I ask in confusion. "Don't I deserve to be happy?"

Surprises and Pain

"Hearing your complaints, I think I'll run a few tests, but first let's do a physical exam," says my Nurse Practitioner.

Her brow wrinkles as she proceeds with the exam. "You're not pregnant are you?"

"I better not be!" I exclaim. "My husband will freak out!"

"Your uterus is a little large. I'm going to run a pregnancy test just to be sure."

She sends me to the restroom with a cup. After placing the completed test in the designated area I wait in the hallway.

"Oops," says the nurse a she saunters into the hall with my results.

I am speechless as I process the implications of what she has conveyed in one simple word.

"You know we can take care of this if you think it will be a problem for your marriage."

I am appalled at her suggestion! No matter how inconvenient this pregnancy might be I would never terminate it! In my mind I feel like shouting at her, but I remain calm, "No, it will be fine. Thanks."

I head home, my mind preparing for how Matt will take the news.

"What?!" He exclaims. "How did this happen? I can't do another baby!"

Though an expected reaction, I am annoyed with his irritation—like he had nothing to do with it!!

We have only been in our new home for about five months and the hardships have been continual. Moving in itself is stressful, but just a few months after the move I discovered some lifestyle choices of Matt's that he'd been hiding because he knew I wouldn't agree with them and the example they would present to the kids. Now an unplanned pregnancy is my reality and the thought of doing it alone overwhelms me to exhaustion.

Matt doesn't say another word.

Feeling rejected, I leave the room.

As my pregnancy progresses I am consumed by nausea. I can barely stand and walk I am so sick, and when I do get up I feel dangerously dizzy and my face turns sheet white. I haven't passed out yet, but wouldn't be surprised if I did. It's hard to even do simple household tasks like laundry and preparing meals, which doesn't help my marriage.

My pregnancy becomes difficult as the months pass on. I am both nervous and excited for this baby. I had always wanted a third child, but didn't think I would ever get to have one. Now I get the opportunity and Matt is even more distant and withdrawn than before. He is not the only one having to adapt to changed plans. What about me? What about the sacrifice of pregnancy? I am feeling the effects of all this right now! He doesn't really have to cope until the birth. Where is compassion? Will he ever come around? Be supportive? Helpful? Or am I destined to feel completely alone for the rest of my life?

The last few months of my pregnancy bring a lot of pain. Sometimes I can barely walk; I hurt so badly. Finally, I am at my last prenatal check-up. My back has been hurting pretty bad all morning. As I sit up after my exam I yelp in pain.

My doctor looks concerned, asks me to describe my pain and checks me again.

"What you've just described to me is worrisome Jennifer, characteristic of a dangerous infection of the amniotic fluid. We need to observe you for a bit."

A short while later I am hooked up to an I.V. and baby monitor. The hours drag on as my pain continues. I begin having contractions. The doctor gives me a shot of Terbutaline to stop them and eventually checks me into the labor and delivery unit. A full blood panel is ordered. I am given a CT scan and sonogram tests. They shoot me up with multiple pain killers and finally, in the middle of the night, after my second shot of Morphine, the pain subsides.

The doctor deliberates regarding induction and orders amniocentesis, but the test results show that the baby's lungs are not developed enough to deliver him.

Finally, pain gone, I ask to be sent home.

Two weeks later we are scheduled for an induction. The baby is due in a week but I have big babies (Kale was 10lbs) and I don't want to risk repeating the drama and pain of the past. I'm not 20 years old anymore!

I feel uneasy for several days before the induction and especially uneasy the morning of, but I go ahead with plans as scheduled.

The doctor starts by breaking my water. We wait for an hour but nothing happens. She starts me on Pitocin and the contractions finally start—hard and close together, sudden and intense, not like my natural labors which always built in intensity. I scream with each contraction, gripping the bed rails.

An hour passes by and no progress has been made. In order to cope, I ask for an epidural.

The anesthesiologist enters the room and hands me a clipboard filled with papers and a lot of fine print.

"What does this say?" I ask.

"It's just a list of all the risks, but they never happen." He hands me the pen.

I sign the papers and sit up so he can insert the needle.

"Wow, you've got a perfect epidural back," the anesthesiologist says as he runs his finger down my spine.

"Can I watch?" Matt asks as he moves to the opposite side of the bed. He has always had a fascination with medical procedures.

The anesthesiologist proceeds to insert the needle in my back, but pulls it out again, "I threaded the vein. Sorry. That's not a good thing, so we'll just try again." His voice sounds nonchalant.

He inserts the needle a second time with the same negative results. "Um, we're gonna need to do it one more time," he says with an embarrassed tone.

"Okay, I think we've got it," he says after the third try. His voice doesn't sound convincing to me and questions about his competence flash through my mind.

I lay back down as he flips the switch on the I.V. to allow the anesthesia to enter my bloodstream. Seconds later my vision blurs and I feel strange, like the room is being pulled away from me.

Nurses scramble around. "Her blood pressure is dropping fast and I can't get a reading on her pulse."

The words sound far away, like they're in a funnel.

"I'll call Dr. Stafford," someone says. "Her blood pressure is 0 over 40. That can't be right! Can it?"

I feel all my extremities begin to tingle, like they have fallen asleep. I recognize the feeling as shock. I have felt it before.

The medical staff seems unnecessarily preoccupied with the machines that measure mine and the baby's stats. I feel dizzy. Am I dying?

As I linger on the edge of consciousness I see Matt's face. Though it seems distant and fuzzy it is decidedly filled with concern and fear. He doesn't want to lose me.

A sudden and intense feeling seizes my chest. It feels like it's going to explode. I've never felt such pain. Am I having a heart attack?! The feeling expands in my chest and I clutch at my heart gasping for air and yelling an indistinguishable sound akin to "Ouuuuuuuch."

The nurses seem helpless; they just stare.

Dr. Stafford enters the room and takes control, "Why isn't she on oxygen? Turn her over on her side. What's going on here?"

As the nurses fill her in my mom, who came to see the delivery, is brought into the room, "What did you give her?" I hear her ask one of the nurses.

I can't hear the nurse's response, but I can hear my mom loud and clear. "She can't have that drug! Why didn't anyone check her paperwork before you started all this?!"

The medical staff has almost succeeded in killing me twice in the last 15 minutes and I am weary and wanting all the conversations and drama to disappear.

"Let's get this little guy here quick, without a C-section. Okay?" Says Dr. Stafford once I am stable.

I nod in exhausted agreement.

Within 30 minutes my son, Brett is in my arms. And for the first time in years I feel like Matt actually cares about me.

Dark Addiction Revealed

Sleepless nights and pure exhaustion are the hallmark of a new baby, but this is crazy. I have been up with Brett seven times a night for a whole year . . . with no help from Matt. The only way I have been able to get any sleep is to let Brett sleep with us, right between Matt and me.

How symbolic.

The inkling of love I saw in the Labor and Delivery room was fleeting and Matt and I have grown even further apart over the last year. I have turned my focus back toward my children and toward healing, knowing I cannot change anything but myself.

I've been reading a book called *Women Who Love Too Much* by Robin Norwood. Unfortunately, I found myself in this book. It is a hard thing to see and acknowledge the ugly truth within, but when we don't see our darkest addictions we can't heal them.

According to this book, I am co-dependent, which basically means I am addicted to my relationship with Matt in an unhealthy way.

I was introduced to co-dependency about three years ago by a marriage therapist, but the material he gave me focused on co-dependency as a result of alcoholic situations, so I had a hard time identifying with it. The woman who wrote this book introduces other reasons for manifestations of co-dependency. As I studied her words, I saw myself and now finally understand the root of this addiction's growth, how I was unknowingly prepared to become co-dependent as a child and how my marriage nurtured those seeds into full-blown issues.

This is a startling revelation for me and has led to much self-reflection and journaling. My addiction of trying to please Matt, trying to solve all our problems, trying to become what he wants (or what I think he wants) keeps me distracted from having to face my own issues—the things I hate about myself, the things I have created and become through my own perceptions and choices. Co-dependency makes the entire situation worse. It is the darkest addiction in my soul.

I have wrestled with many feelings this morning. I feel shame for being so out of control in my life and having a problem like co-dependency. I never thought of myself as being the kind of person who could suffer from a compulsion like this. I feel truly humbled and miserable.

I have been thinking about my childhood and family, and have identified some generational patterns of co-dependency. One grandparent was the spouse of an alcoholic. The seeds of co-dependency are manifest in the lives of many of their children. The other side of the family didn't have any obvious co-dependent behaviors, but a pattern of unhealthy self-sacrifice is evident to varying degrees. In addition to these genetic factors, my childhood experiences pre-disposed me to the need for approval and other dysfunctions.

Dr. Norwood's book includes a chart of the progression of co-dependency and healing. I have struggled with many of the points on her downward chart, but not all. I find myself at the very bottom of the recovery curve. I pray God will give me the strength and show me the way to break this addiction and become healthy again.

Life-Altering Decision

There are moments that determine your life path, commitments that define you, choices that leave you changed for having made them. Tonight feels like one of those moments.

I went to a women's networking meeting the other night for a business I am trying to start. The guest speaker was a former Mrs. Utah. I have known for the last several weeks that she was coming to speak. I even drove through a horrible snow storm to hear her speak, and I hate driving in the snow. I felt compelled to hear her message, though I couldn't explain why. But after hearing her I understood. Everything she said felt like a direct and personal message prepared just for me. Ever since then, I haven't been able to shake this feeling of needing to compete in a pageant. This is the third time I have felt this feeling. I don't think it's a coincidence that everything she said was exactly what I needed to hear, and by the time she was done speaking I knew what I had to do.

I have decided to do a pageant next year. I wrote this goal down and told three trusted individuals that I am doing it. I haven't told Matt yet. He will think it is stupid and won't understand. I don't even get it. I just know I need to do it.

I find it interesting that the year I compete (next year) will be three years from the last time I made this goal (and then tore up the paper because I decided not to do it). I don't know what to expect from all of this. Naturally, I am nervous but I can't deny this repetitive "call" to participate in this particular event. I wish I knew the purpose of all this.

Fearing People's Opinions

On Sundays, I teach the 12- and 13-year old girls at church. The curriculum for today incorporated an object lesson that included a flower in a pot. I didn't really have any flowers growing, nor did I have a nice pot so I did what I could and took what I had. Perhaps if I had left myself more time to prepare my lesson, I wouldn't have had to settle for a lame visual, but it seems my emotional healing journey is sucking up every ounce of available energy, and I am just skating by in many areas of my life.

Every teacher had the same lesson today for their individual classes, and when I walked into opening exercises (where we meet before splitting into classes), one of the other teachers was holding a beautiful blue and yellow ceramic pot in the shape of a teacup with a lovely, lush flower growing out from the center of it. I looked at my limp and puny flower in its clay pot and shrunk in my seat, feeling inadequate. I pushed it under my chair with my foot hoping nobody had noticed it.

Yesterday, I made a Jell-o salad for a funeral. When I poured it out of the mold, I realized that I didn't have any whipping cream for decorating it. It seemed lacking somehow, even more so when I put it on a disposable foam plate (so I wouldn't have to worry about getting my dishes back since I didn't know the family). As I handed it over to the kitchen committee, I felt insecure, like my Jell-o was somehow inadequate. On the walk home worries of freezer burned fruit danced through my head. What if it tastes yucky? What if they hate it? What if they know I made it?

Last Sunday, I didn't share some information in my Family History class because I was afraid I would blush while I was speaking (I do that a lot) and that would embarrass me further. I'm a hopeless cause. What am I thinking entering a pageant?!!!!

I constantly feel like I'm being judged, like I'm under scrutiny. Part of that is because Matt constantly criticizes everything I do. He probably thinks he is offering helpful information to me—information that he believes will help me be better and more efficient—but his approach leaves me feeling like I am never good enough for him. Sometimes I feel like he hates me. In many ways he has become the biggest adversary I have ever known. But I am just as bad to myself. In fact, I've heard it said that we only allow others to abuse us to the level we abuse ourselves. I judge myself; criticize myself quicker and more harshly than anyone else. It's my buffer. If I beat other people to the criticisms I believe are coming, it won't hurt so much.

The further I get into preparing for the pageant the more demons I see in myself, the harder I have to fight and the more energy is consumed in the fighting. In the process of healing, it seems like things get worse before they get better. I hate that. I am hindered at every turn with baggage. I can't believe I carry so much darkness, so much insecurity and so little personal power. No wonder I'm unhappy.

Healing the heart requires an education in personal faults and weaknesses. Only in acquiring awareness of these things can I change them, but the process is so discouraging, so disheartening at times. I feel like a shattered porcelain doll and no amount of glue can fix me.

Faltering

A year passes quickly. I have written in notebook after notebook, examining my passions and life purpose, trying to discover the perfect platform for the pageant. I have asked myself questions in an attempt to get to know who I am and to prepare for the Interview portion of the competition. I have stretched my comfort zone, created a group for teen girls where I organized meetings and provided guest speakers for them. I have acquired sponsors and sought out my perfect "look" for the pageant. I have practiced my swimsuit and evening gown "walks". I even hired a coach and spent six months in guided growth and pageant preparation. It has been exhausting and intense.

Today I walk across the padded floor of a local dance studio; following the pattern I have been shown. We are practicing evening gown walk—all 25 contestants.

One week to go! It is crunch time.

Every woman is checking out her competition, it can't be helped. I feel a wash of discouragement and despair as I survey the room of beautiful women. I have no right to be here. I am not pageant material. My puny supply of confidence slips away by the second. I try to fake it, but I am failing miserably. I straighten my spine and walk as elegantly as I can, but it's hard when you know your competition (many whom have done this very thing numerous times) are all staring at you and weighing your strengths and weaknesses.

I feel ridiculous and have no clue what I look like because we are facing away from the mirrors on the wall.

"You're upper body is too stiff," the choreographer whispers to me as she pulls me aside after my run-through. She shows me what it should look like. I can't seem to grasp how to hold myself with good posture and not appear stiff.

I watch the other women walk. I pick out a few sure contenders for the crown. They are so elegant and so confident. They take their time strutting across the floor. I am discouraged. I know I am not the only one. By the end of the day, three ladies have dropped out of the competition.

So far, all of the workshops I have attended have been sit-down-and-listen, instructional-type events, with a little bit of time for socializing afterwards. Those have been really nice and I sincerely love all the women I've met, but today I feel off and jealous.

I feel lousy the entire day. By evening, I know that I am dealing with more than just a case of jittery nerves and insecurities. I am getting sick. My throat is sore and I ache everywhere.

I remember the day after Thanksgiving. I was decorating the Christmas tree, like I always do. As I strung the tinsel garland around the branches I suddenly felt bewildered, "What the heck am I doing?" I asked myself. "This is the dumbest thing I have ever tried to do. Who am I to enter a beauty pageant?" A palpable loss of motivation left my body that day and I haven't been able to get it back since. Compound that with today's barrage of insecurities and impending illness, and I am in no shape for competition.

My marriage has been steadily declining, my self-worth vacillating. In February, some pretty major blows hit my marriage and since that time I have been in a cloud of confusion. I've been drowning in loss, unable to fully recover. That abyss has completely contracted around me and permeated every aspect of my life. Like a lung, it sometimes expands and I feel a little lighter, but I am quickly submerged and constricted again in stress and struggle.

I feel fat, ugly and totally out of my league today. Everything I thought I had going for me was shown up by the other women who had it even better than I. I don't feel like I have any strengths going into this thing. Without the feelings of love and light, I am nothing and that is really all I had. Anyone can be graceful, poised and elegant with practice. There is nothing unique and special about me. My efforts to reconnect with God seem futile. Why does it feel like light cannot enter my soul? Perhaps I lost the light the moment my faith gave way to doubt about the purpose for this process and my participation in it. Perhaps it was my doubting that God could make anything of me. Maybe doubting that I matter did it. Isn't fear my overall life challenge? Isn't that the thing I struggle most to defeat? I have never grasped opportunity or dreams because of fear. It controls me. I guess deep down at this moment I don't believe I can be a Mrs. Utah, so why bother.

Interview

I pull my Honda into the parking lot of the performance center and fix my hair and lipstick in the rear-view mirror. My heels clack on the pavement as I walk up the stairs to the offices where preliminary pageant interviews are being held. I try and calm the twisting anxiety in my stomach with a deep breath, but I can't seem to subdue it.

"Go over there and get your picture taken," the director says, "then come back in here until your contestant number is called. After your interview, you are not allowed to talk to anyone except us." She points to the assistant director. "Come and grab a gift basket when you are done and then leave the building. We will see you tomorrow morning at eight." She smiles.

I wait; visiting a bit with the other contestants in my group, but everyone is pretty quiet and focused, so I take a seat in the foyer. A contestant comes out of the interview room and starts sobbing. I know I shouldn't talk to her but I am concerned. I follow her into the restroom and wait for her to come out of one of the stalls. I fix my hair but she still doesn't emerge so I exit, sitting back down in the foyer.

"Are you okay?" I ask when she finally comes out and walks past me. She talks to me for a bit, keeping her remarks very generic and assuring me that she is okay—that her tears are just a release of anxiety and emotion from being so nervous beforehand.

The director spots us talking and asks her to leave. I am left alone again with my thoughts. I had appreciated the distraction.

My turn creeps closer. I am second to last. I am not sure what to expect; my stomach turns in little flips at the unknown. I pace back and forth, waiting.

"Contestant 20," the assistant director finally calls.

I step to the double-door and exhale slowly.

"You'll have five minutes" she says. "Don't sit down until invited to do so and don't shake hands. Answer the questions the best you can, and when you hear the word *Time*, wrap up your statement, thank the judges and walk out the door."

I nod in understanding.

The door opens and I enter to face five strangers about whom I know nothing, but who have read my Bio and have a list of questions they want to ask me.

The firing begins as questions shoot from left and right. I speak and feel suddenly calm. I had asked God for the miracle of being able to relax during the interviews and my request has been granted. I am surprised at how easy the questions are to answer; I thought they would be more difficult.

I shouldn't have thought that.

I suddenly get a question for which I hadn't prepared.

"Can I tell you a story?" I ask, stalling for time.

"Of course," says the judge who asked the question, as she leans forward on her elbows in anticipation.

"Once upon a time there was a girl . . ." I begin my story about a girl who had to face shape-shifting dragons that attacked her, and how she ran from these dragons until she realized that she had the power to fight back.

By the time I finish the story my brain has grasped how to tie it into the question she posed.

The judges seem happy with my response.

I smile.

"Time," calls the assistant director.

"Is there anything else you'd like to add before we end?" One judge asks.

"No, I think that's it," I say. "Thank you for your time."

I exit the room. "That was so fun!" I tell the assistant director.

"You did great," she says.

The next morning I find out that many of the contestants were asked the same final question: Is there anything else you'd like to add? I find out that the correct answer to that question is to re-state why you are qualified to be Mrs. Utah, followed by an expression of passion for your platform. A little oomph goes out of my sail as I realize I bombed my final question, but I can't change it now.

Into the Lion's Den

It is 9:00 o'clock on competition morning and we have been sitting around for over an hour because a pipe broke at the performance center, flooding the stage area, causing problems for our set. I'm worried. Right now we should be practicing the opening number routine we learned a few days ago. Fortunately, we finally migrate to a dance studio in the building.

As we practice our walks and opening number routine I feel a sense of self-esteem and confidence that didn't exist at our last rehearsal. Gratitude for this change washes over me.

Although I am not a competitive person, performance has always had a way of making me climb higher and access energy that I can't seem to find in rehearsals. Still, as we approach show time and I see that some women suddenly and miraculously have a full head of luxurious hair that reaches their waists, I can't help but compare myself to them. Why didn't anyone tell me about those kinds of extensions?! I feel like I'm playing a game but I don't know all the rules. It feels a little unfair.

"Show time ladies," a voice shouts into the air.

Our stage is phenomenal. The Utah State Opera donated an incredible set with entrances on either side of the stage and a curved staircase for us to walk down (in our heels of course). It is both beautiful and foreboding. The house is full, over 700 people are in the audience and a camera crew is recording the event.

I am no stranger to the stage, and although I have always been a bit of a nervous performer, I have never been a nervous dancer, except tonight. I can't seem to stop shaking. I feel unnatural, stiff and jittery as we move through the opening number. My smile feels like plaster, heavy and fake.

As the number rounds to a close, I move to center stage with the final two contestants. I strike the pose I'm supposed to take and in the process, feel a rhinestone from one of my heels snag and rip my nylons on the inside of my calf. I continue with the number as if nothing happened.

"Crap," I whisper as I run back to the dressing room when the number is over. "Now I have to re-glue a new pair of pantyhose to my body."

This is not a rapid task. Once you rub the glue on your torso, you have to wait for it to get tacky before you can stick your nylons to it. With the waistband of the stocking removed it's important to do this so your nylons stay on, and so your wardrobe (especially the swimsuit) is seamless and sleek.

When able, I dive into my swimsuit, change my heels to a strappy, nude-colored, four-inch style and wait in the wings for my turn to descend the precarious 9-step staircase. As I climb the stairs back-stage, one of my heels gets caught on the edge of a stair.

"Contestant number 20." The emcee's voice booms through the speakers.

Adrenaline floods my body. The director has already explained that if anyone misses their turn, they miss their turn. End of story. And my shoe is stuck!!

I grab hold of my ankle, jerk my foot free, step onto the stage and descend the stairs as if nothing had happened . . . again. The adrenaline serves as a good distraction from nerves and I feel like I *own* my swimsuit walk, which is a huge breakthrough for me! I have always felt so self-conscious in a swimsuit.

Thankfully, nothing eventful happens as I prepare for the evening gown competition, though it's this part of the competition that makes me most nervous. This is when the husbands join their wives for their onstage walk. Not understanding the purpose of the pageant, Matt has fought me on this journey the whole way, and it's a miracle he's even here with me tonight.

When I emerge from the dressing room, he is standing with some of the other husbands backstage. He looks happy to see me, but uncomfortable. I walk toward him, passing several couples who are gazing romantically into each other's eyes. As our eyes meet, I can't help but feel like something is missing. We've been through a lot these past few months and in many ways, I haven't recovered from the devastating blows of choice his actions have dealt to our relationship. It seems as if he isn't proud to be there with me, like the other husbands seem to be with their wives. He doesn't say otherwise so I let his silence confirm my assumptions. It feels like his presence is out of resignation, not support. He has always felt that if the odds are against you, usually it isn't worth the investment of time or money to do it. Twenty-to-one odds are not that great for the financial, time and emotional investments I have made in this pageant. In the back of my mind, I feel that if I fail tonight, his hurtful words from over a decade ago will be justified in my loss—proof that I really am ugly and a loser.

We get through Evening Gown and intermission comes. I am standing in the dressing room, and like many of the contestants, practicing responses to the on-stage question that will be asked of the ten lucky finalists who advance to the next level of competition. I start to review my potential answers but suddenly feel like it won't matter what I say so I put my questions away.

Fifteen minutes later, 21 women stand on the stage in rows on the stairs waiting for the results of the top ten. The moment passes like a dream. I can't seem to process the fact that all ten names have been called and mine was not among them.

Dazed, I make my way back to the dressing room trying to grasp what just happened. Tears fill the corners of my eyes; I blink them back. My phone beeps with a text from my son stating that he had a feeling that I wasn't going to get in the top ten, even though he hoped I would. He says my daughter is crying and everybody is bored and wants to leave since I am not going to be in the rest of the competition. I swallow hard. It hurts to have disappointed everyone so badly.

The next morning, I am exhausted, tearful, pathetic and a million other indistinguishable emotions. I had prepared so hard for so long, pushed through so much emotional garbage, and for what?

At the last workshop, the director told us not to have a goal, not even the top ten. She didn't want anyone to be devastated. I don't feel devastated, but certainly shaken up. I really had convinced myself that I could at least make the top ten. I feel foolish now for ever believing that.

Why am I not good enough to be in the top ten? I already knew I wasn't beautiful; did that point really need to be driven home? Part of me feels like giving up on myself and my talents. What's the point? I feel a loss of focus, disorientation, confusion, and disappointment. I know I will be okay. I always am, but why did I feel so strongly that I needed to do this pageant? Was I delusional enough to believe that somehow I might actually win the crown?

I have been through hell since Thanksgiving and I don't feel like any of it was worth it. Right now, I don't feel like the benefits outweigh the challenges. In this moment, life sucks.

Understanding

Today I received an email from the director with the scores from the pageant. I am amazed as I review and see what actually occurred during the competition. I performed better than I thought. I placed sixth in the preliminary interviews and third in swimsuit, which is a total shocker to me! But I placed tenth in Evening Gown. Tenth! I bombed. My judge's comments say my dress is gorgeous, but I am a little stiff. So what gives? Why tenth?

A few weeks later I get the video from pageant night and can see why I did so poorly in the evening gown competition. I am not just stiff, I lack radiance. I am not smiling and look unhappy to be on that stage. I suppose my countenance is directly related to the insecure and troublesome thoughts and feelings I had backstage with Matt, and just moments before I walked out. Words, whether spoken, thought or felt have a powerful impact on the countenance and presence.

It makes sense now. Had I embraced joy and allowed my true light to shine forth regardless of my beliefs about Matt's feelings, I probably would have made the top ten since overall I only missed it by two spots. The ultimate outcome of the pageant would not have changed but I would have experienced my desired outcome (to be in the top ten). I really did have some control over how things turned out but because I let my negative beliefs and fears become queen I ended up wearing the crown of disappointment.

A week later I attend a going-away party for the director who is moving to another state. I get to know many of the pageant contestants better, sans competition, and find them to be incredibly inspirational. They are so passionate about life and their causes, really firm in the knowledge of who they are and what they can accomplish. They know where their personal power lies. They are purpose-driven, clear in their intentions, motivated and focused. They network and know how to get others excited about their crusades. I want this kind of power for myself!

I am being invited, through their example, to step up and live a new way—to join their ranks. I have received an invitation to greatness, as every woman does, and it doesn't look like I thought it would. I don't need a crown to have impact in this world.

I go home and pull out my guitar, a song comes quickly. *I'm a powerful voice. I'm an untapped vision. I am beauty. I am love* . . . it's an affirmation of self-worth for me and every woman.

Several weeks pass. I find more peace each day with the outcome of the pageant. I realize that I am stronger in many ways for having competed.

Book III

Caterpillar on the Beach

"How does one become a butterfly? She asked pensively. You must want to fly so much that you are willing to give up being a caterpillar."
~Trina Paulus

Missed Opportunity

My stomach tingles with bubbles of anticipation. I lean across Matt and look out the window below as we circle around the island in preparation for landing. I take some pictures through the window and ask my two-year-old son, Brett, if he can say *Maui*.

As we exit the plane and enter the outdoor airport, the island humidity embraces us. Like a warm hug from an old friend, I feel instantly at home. Everything is so inviting and somehow familiar here. There is an absence of pretense as refreshing and inviting as a cold glass of lemonade on a hot afternoon. I feel immediately welcome. It's not that anyone is particularly friendly to us. Everyone is busy with their own lives, baggage and transportation. I simply feel an inexplicable sense of belonging here, as if I have come home to a long forgotten place.

We pick up our luggage and head toward the shuttle that takes us to the rental car building. It takes nearly an hour to get our car. After almost seven hours on a plane who wants to sit around waiting for a car so they can get in it for *another* hour to drive to the resort? I just want to be there already! I've got an island sunset to watch in a few hours. It's one of my greatest desires. I don't know why but I feel a deep need to sit on the shore near the water and watch the sun set in peaceful splendor. Probably because I have just come through all the craziness of last month's pageant and I could use some serious serenity.

Finally we get to our condo! But we still haven't really arrived because we need food. So Matt and I hop back in the car and head to the nearest grocery store where we push a cart up and down unfamiliar aisles for another hour trying to find what we need. I'm getting restless, my shoulder muscles are tensing. Sunset is approaching and I'm stuck in the grocery store!

All too soon Chelsey calls me from the condo and says, "You're missing the sunset! It's almost over and it's amazing!"

I knew it was late, but not that late, or at least I hoped it wasn't. It feels like springs are winding in my legs and I want to sprint out of the store to get a glimpse at the fading sky, but I know we still have so much left to do. I let out a heavy sigh in an attempt to unwind my muscles and my desires. The urge finally passes. Disappointment and responsibility are my companions right now. They frequently are.

It's well after dark when we return to the condo. I pour everybody a bowl of cold cereal for dinner because it's too late to cook. I clean up the kitchen with a heavy heart. Months of anticipation and I had missed my first chance to see an island sunset. I know I have six more nights, but I didn't want any of those nights to go to waste. By 1:00 o'clock in the morning, everyone is asleep and I'm exhausted. I lay down. At least the bed is comfortable.

Unrest Rising

What a beautiful morning! I am finally looking out at the ocean from the shoreline! The joy I feel at this moment melts away any trace of disappointment I felt at last night's missed opportunity. The early morning sun warms my back as Matt, Kale and Chelsey make friends with the water. Brett sits next to me on the sand. He thinks the water is "scary, scary," so he watches from afar, perfectly content to sit calmly at my side, squishing the sand between his toes and fingers.

This morning we all woke up early, wanting to head to the beach before breakfast. The walk from our condo was about a mile long but nobody complained. It didn't feel that far since there was so much to take in. The meandering path that led to the shore wound through an emerald-colored golf course lined with flowering shrubbery, Plumeria and palm trees. Chelsey gathered fallen flowers as we walked, while Brett chased birds and squealed with delight as they fluttered away from him. The words *beautiful* and *breathtaking* kept coming to my mind as I gazed at the endless azure sky and felt the indescribable silence in the air, creating a profound sense of peace in my soul.

I have never been to Maui before and yet I feel such a connection with this place. I felt it the moment I stepped off the plane. Why? As I walked toward the beach a few minutes ago, soaking up the early morning sunshine, I was seized by a sudden and intense desire to move to the island. I am in love with this place and never want to leave! I suppose most people feel that way in paradise. What is it about this place that makes me feel so at home? How is this place able to instantaneously grip my emotions and command my devotion? Is it novelty? Is it beauty? Or is it something more?

I currently live at an elevation slightly higher than 4,600 feet. I grew up at an elevation of 25 feet. My physical orientation to the sea shifted eight years ago when I moved from California to Utah. Upon arriving in Maui, my soul instantly recognized this detail and immediately directed my body to settle into the familiar feeling of a low sea level. It took concentrated mental effort on my part to pinpoint this connection on a conscious level. I suppose this awareness takes a little magic out of the feeling, but understanding the connection is helpful in knowing why I feel so drawn to the island.

How often do our souls recognize what our conscious mind does not? How often do we desire, or long for something and not really understand why we feel the way we do? How often do we act without really understanding why we are acting? How often do we feel discontent in our current condition, simply because we do not recognize our underlying longings or their origin?

There is a difference between something being right and something feeling comfortable, good, or familiar. Maui feels comfortable to me because it mimics the physical environment of my youth—a time when I was carefree and flourishing. My childhood days were healthier times for me in so many ways. I long to feel that way again. Because of this subconscious association with past experiences, I instantly feel healthier and safer in Maui. It just feels right here and I never want to go back home. Period. However, as I reflect on these things, I come to see that my longing to stay in this place doesn't make a move here practical or right. In fact, the longer I consider the possibility, the more I realize that moving here would not be the best thing for either me or my family. Separating what is right or best from that which feels familiar and comfortable is not always easy. It takes a lot of effort to understand why we feel drawn to something so strongly. To act from that sensation alone can leave us with regrets. Still the longing is intense. It is difficult to deny the very thing you associate with joy, health, love, youth and other emotions I'm associating with this island.

This new knowledge leaves me a bit depressed. In one short week, I will exchange this new-found—or rediscovered—sensation of belonging for my chaotic, unfulfilling life back in the dry desert of Utah. The prospect seems about as unsavory as a piece of stale bread. Perhaps visiting Maui was a mistake. I didn't come here to be filled with discontent and a longing that I know will never be fulfilled. Feeling the desirably familiar and knowing that I cannot keep it fills me with dissatisfaction. Maui was meant to be a gift. Where is the gift in that?

The beach is fairly empty this morning. I watch passersby as they stroll along the shore. They all seem so happy and carefree. Of course! It's beautiful here! How can they not be happy? How can I not be happy? I *should* be happy, but I'm not, and that makes me feel even more discontent. I'm sitting on the most beautiful beach I have ever seen in a tropical paradise having my own private pity party. How sad! And yet, even sadder is the fact that I sense within me something deeper at play than just discontent with where I live. I sense the ugliness of repressed emotional garbage.

I force myself to focus on the beautiful moment of sand and sunshine before me, but I can't shake the yucky feeling I have right now. I know all too well that unresolved emotions rise again and again until they have been acknowledged and addressed, and I don't want them to ruin my vacation. I close my eyes for a moment, take a deep breath, and reopen my eyes to the glistening water and clear horizon. Too bad my heart isn't as still as the sea this morning.

Pain in the Silence

Except for some beautiful scenery on our drive this morning, it's been a miserable day for me. I feel like crap. It seemed like such a nice thing to take a Sunday drive on the famous Road to Hana, but it was awful. Can't vacations ever just be peaceful? Why do they always have to include arguments and stress?!

The drive was longer than we anticipated and Brett was cranky and irritable. When we finally found the first stop at Twin Falls, it was crowded with people. We had to park pretty far from the entrance and walk along the highway to enter the park. Because it was high noon and intensely humid, Chelsey and Kale were complaining and fighting with each other. By the time we arrived at the first waterfall, we were all so irritated with each other that we decided to head back to the car. It just wasn't worth it. This is when things began to get really ugly for me.

It started yesterday. Matt shared a casual opinion with me at the beach. It wasn't directed at me, but of course I found a way to turn it back on myself and be offended by his words. I am a master at that. I started feeling bad about myself and, as a result, resurrected some old insecurities, things I thought I had healed.

Apparently not.

Still harboring those feelings of rejection, we reached the exit of the park and paused by a Smoothie Shack. It was the only source of liquid refreshment for miles and we hadn't brought any water with us. Brett was screaming from fatigue and over-stimulation, his cheeks red from the heat. I suggested that we buy smoothies for the kids. Matt and I argued for a few minutes about the price of the drinks and finally he gave in. Ten minutes passed and we hadn't even moved an inch in line. I was about to scream!

Something akin to Mount St. Helen's began building up inside me and I was about to blow. Chelsey and Kale were still complaining as Brett struggled with all his might to free himself from my arms. I glared at Matt standing coolly off to the side of the line, seemingly unaffected by everything that was going on. How could he be so blind? Here I was struggling with the kids and he just stood there like a stranger! Exasperated, I thrust Brett into his arms and demanded that we leave.

Like ants, we headed single-file down the highway back to the car. I trailed behind everyone else. My fuse has blown, but in a silent way. Anger surged through my body. I was angry because our outing had been so miserable. I was angry with the kids for arguing. I was angry with Matt for being a miser when we were so obviously parched. I was angry because he hadn't helped me with the kids. I was angry about his comments on the beach yesterday. I was angry with the smoothie shack operator for moving like a snail. I was angry with my pathetic life. I was angry with myself for my insecurities, fears and inability to change the things I struggled for years to change. I found myself in a moment of sheer overwhelming emotion.

A sudden irrational thought seized me. *What if I jump out into the on-coming traffic and end my misery*? The thought existed for about a quarter of second, but in that fraction of an instant, it felt real and intense. I was surprised by the thought. I am not a suicidal person. And though angry and overly emotional, I was rational enough to recognize it for what it was—an irrational thought. Just a thought and one I would never act on. I chastised myself for even allowing such a thought to manifest in my consciousness. But at the same time, I felt such a complete and indescribable need to escape my life and my feelings that I couldn't stand it. Hitting critical mass, my emotions, like the heat and humidity, had become unbearable.

I climbed into the car and barely spoke. Matt suggested we stop at the store on the way back to the condo. I could have cared less about groceries at that moment. I just wanted to crumple up in a little ball and disappear, leaving my reality in the dust.

We drove in silence for much of the car ride. The air conditioning cooled my body and my emotions. I noticed a little roadside fruit stand and insisted that we stop and get something. The owner cut up a fresh island pineapple for us and we snacked on the juice-packed wedges as we drove along the highway. Sweet mercy! Finally something good! It was amazing what a drop in temperature and a little liquid refreshment did for all our emotions!

We finally reached the store and it was a madhouse. We drove around the parking lot for 15 minutes before we could even find a parking spot. Inside the store was even worse, so crowded I felt like a sardine in a can. We had to guide our cart with extreme precision to avoid colliding with other shoppers. I've seen crowded shopping centers, but never this bad. I have never been so glad to leave a store.

It is late afternoon now. My sweet toddler is asleep beside me as I sit on my unmade bed. I have been reflecting on my disturbing experience this morning and am still troubled by it. What is going on? Why this sudden rush of negative and irrational emotion? Why now?

The silence speaks the answer to my heart.

With no phone calls, no media devices, no appointments, no projects, no yard or housework, no marathon-type pageant preparation, I'm forced to face the emotions and pain that I have been stifling for so long. I have no distractions here to save me from myself. The lack of busyness has created space in my life and all of the fed up, numb, frustrated, angry and unhappy aspects of my life are raising their voices and demanding to be heard. They no longer have to compete with anything. I am their captive. I am forced to listen to what my soul has to say.

A sense of the wasted years washes over me. I feel my mistakes acutely. I feel regret. I must not be worthy of anything good. I must not be worthy of happiness, let alone worthy of a sense of accomplishment and success. Self-disgust begs for release. The desire to escape beats heavily inside my chest, rising up to my head until it begins to ache. I don't want to stop living; I just want to stop living a crappy life. What can I do? I am desperate to find a solution that rids me of these feelings.

I weigh my options. What if I stay in Maui, send my family home and start a new life for myself? What if I leave Matt and wipe the slate of relationship mistakes clean? What if I just continue on with my pathetic life as it is? What if I make the wrong decision? Will I survive the consequences of my actions? What if I can't change things? What will that mean for me? Will I be doomed to a life of unhappiness and misery? What if? What if? What if?

My seeming lack of attachment to my family appalls me as I explore my options. I censure myself. I love my family profoundly. I just feel wretched and desperate for a solution that will bring peace and freedom. Physical escape seems the obvious and only solution at this point. What am I to do? I can't keep feeling this way. I can't.

Surrounded by beauty on every side, the ugliness in my soul emerges like a wound, begging to be treated and healed. I am not what I should be. I am not even close to my ideal. No matter how hard I try, how high I reach, I fall short. I am pathetic. I am a mess. Thank goodness, I brought a book with me! Sweet escape! And in the drug of my choice! I bury my head in the pages for the rest of the evening and the following morning until I finish it. Too bad it isn't longer.

The Caterpillar's Dilemma

A caterpillar is an interesting creature. It scoots along, gorging on leaves until it instinctively senses that a change is required. Filled to maximum capacity, it sheds its outer skin by splitting it in two and inching out of it. What is left is a soft, vulnerable chrysalis with the caterpillar inside. This chrysalis hardens in about an hour and over the next 9 to 14 days, the caterpillar transforms into an entirely new creature, emerging with wings, able to fly. Fourteen days doesn't seem like very long for such a complete transformation, but when you consider the fact that the butterfly only has a one-month life span, it's a pretty significant amount of time.

I feel a lot like a caterpillar. I have gorged myself for years on distraction and busyness, trying to stuff down a lifetime of neglected emotions, hurt, regrets and especially rejection. Yesterday, I split. My skin peeled back and revealed a vulnerable, unsightly lump of soul—my soul. I now stand at a crossroads. I can either hang here and rot, or I can inch my way out of this skin and allow nature to run its course. In all honesty, trusting nature to run its course scares me. I don't think I can handle any more pain, but I desperately need to feel release, freedom from the hell of my emotions. But freedom always comes at a price. What toll will she extract from me?

Sunset by the Sea

I sit on a big, black volcanic rock just before sunset. The waves crash beneath me forming foamy, white swirls around the base of the rocks. There is something magical about the sea as orange rays from the setting sun cast playful beams of light across the water. The smell of the sea seems stronger in the evening when the activity of the day subsides. It tickles my nose with salty pleasure. The gentle humidity on my skin, softened by the cool breeze, is welcome compared to the cold, stale air of the condo from where I just came.

There are only a handful of people on the beach—couples, lovers who have come to share the romance of an island sunset. Some try to capture the moment with their cameras. Some hold each other and kiss. A few people, like me, watch alone in silence. There is something so welcoming about the sea at sunset. It beckons and invites all who will listen to hear, to be still.

The sea has a voice. For those who are open to her wisdom, she carries secrets on her breath. Tonight, she tells me I worry too much, that I don't relax or let my guard down enough. She tells me that I am fearful of getting hurt, that I don't trust life. Even as I write, I glance around to make sure that I am safe. Instinctively, I know I am safe, but neurosis rears its ugly head when authenticity is suppressed, and I haven't lived truly authentically since I was a child. Tonight, in the rhythms of the surf, I hear a faint beating. It is my heart but it is so far away. There are so many walls, so many layers of protection smothering my true identity, whatever that is.

My thoughts drift as I inhale and my senses are filled with life. When was the last time I fed my senses? When was the last time I allowed myself to feel wonder? Alone in this perfectly splendid solitude, I am whole. It is a strange, but welcome feeling. I am at peace with myself. I am enough. I am renewed. There is no one crying, no one arguing, no one demanding anything from me. There is no one judging or comparing me. No expectation from the sea or the sand. I can just be me, free and perfect exactly as I am, limitations, faults and all.

The sea doesn't mind. She simply calls me by name, beckons me to stay awhile and invites me to connect with life, become one, fluid in motion, thought and form, at peace I have never felt the sense of beauty and serenity I am feeling right now. The quiet of my bedroom back home doesn't do it. The garden bench in my backyard doesn't do it. I am in love with the sea. I need this. I'm afraid I'll never feel this way again. It's as if I've found something I didn't even know I had lost, and only now, upon rediscovering it, can I see its worth.

For a moment, I have come home to myself. I have somehow bypassed all the pain, issues, regrets and grudges I held inside, and landed right in the middle of my own perfect truth. It is a moment of sheer magic. Why can't I always feel like this? What prevents it? Is it simply geography that makes this feeling possible? Or is it more? Can I re-create this moment in my daily life back home?

I never watch the sunset at home. The power lines and rooftops obscure my view while the rush of trucks on the road and the sound of air conditioning units humming through the dry desert streets disturb the silence. Why bother? From time to time, I have glanced up at the pink and gold sky above the rooftops as the sun descends, and even paused to utter the word "beautiful" at the scene, but the full experience of watching the sun set is marred by the visual obstructions and daily distractions surrounding me.

Today, on this quiet piece of paradise, I understand the full meaning of the word *awe*. I never knew that a sunset, a common everyday occurrence, could instill such a powerful serenity within me. In this moment, the perfectionist voice of self-criticism drowns in the rhythmic lull of the waves. My eyes fix upon the glowing orange disc as it slips between golden clouds and I am swallowed up in the beauty of personal freedom. Suspended in a field of perfect detachment, yet embraced by a sense of wonder and love.

I have never been so still, so at peace. Nor have I felt as perfect as I do in this moment. A perfection that is free from any preconceived definition or judgment. It's as if there's no such thing as judgment at all. I just am. And that is enough. I imagine this experience is akin to what it feels like to be a baby. Free of the confines of definition and the expectations of peers and family. Free to fully experience the wonder and joy of life. A baby is beautiful and perfect, and we allow it to be so until she reaches toddlerhood, at which point we begin placing all kinds of limitations and definitions on her.

Life is complicated and messy. Millions of experiences, messages, choices and perceptions combine to create a life. Like it or not, we are where we are at this present moment. My present moment is exquisite and yet, I know it will end and I will be faced with the ugly reality that I am not happy with my life.

Since arriving on the island, I cannot shake the stark contrast between my overstuffed, lackluster life and the abundant vibrancy that exists here. The belonging and freedom I am feeling, and the moments of bliss I've experienced in these few short days, testify that there's something more, something better, than what I've been living.

How can I create moments like these back home? I certainly cannot pack the seashore in my suitcase and take it with me. An audio recording of the ocean waves doesn't provide the same effect either. There is something about being still and alone in a peaceful setting that allows one to experience release.

Stillness and solitude serve a dual purpose. First, they have the power to call up the myriad of emotions that have been long stuffed and neglected in one's heart; stillness and solitude invite pain. They have visited my heart for the past several days and vividly awakened the suffering in my heart. To experience the second purpose of stillness and solitude pain must first be awakened and acknowledged. Then stillness and solitude become a canvas for moments like these, where peace and clarity can arise spontaneously and invite healing. They allow truth and authenticity to emerge in one's life.

To get to the peace, I must pass through the pain. I must walk right through it, acknowledge it without judgment and move forward toward healing. If I stay in the pain, swimming around in circles as I have done in the past, I will never reach the shores of tranquility and truth. I never understood how to get to this place before. I thought it only existed for other people, not me, yet here it is. To find the true self, even for a few moments, is to connect with the divine, to bypass the flesh and experience something beyond this world. It is to connect with hope. The truth within is the real definition of freedom.

Now that I've tasted liberation, I want to own it and make it mine always. But I don't know how. My life requires that I be involved and engaged in so many ways. I can't ignore responsibility or continually retreat into tranquility for that defeats the purpose of life, which is living. Even continual repose would most likely become stagnant after awhile. I don't want to close myself off from interaction and experience. I am just so bliss-deprived, I am desperate to grab hold of peacefulness and never let it go.

The waves wash up over the sand, back and forth, back and forth. The sea whispers the solution to my soul. Balance is the key, the great yin and yang, the black and white, the high and low, the cycles and seasons. I have always struggled with balance.

What is balance? Balance is simply equilibrium. When we make a concentrated effort toward maintaining balance in life we are assisting equilibrium in this natural tendency toward neutrality, lack of extremes, moderation. Actively seeking to balance rest, relaxation and work is healthy and essential to life. Perhaps my experience today has been so profound because I have an extremely high tolerance for imbalance in my life. I experience no real rest or relaxation, at least not on a deep and nurturing level. I am addicted to working, to doing. There is an incredible difference between the kind of rest and relaxation to which I'm accustomed, the kind that offers distraction from daily cares, and the kind of rest and relaxation that nourishes, nurtures, refreshes. The kind that heals daily cares and instills a sense of renewal within.

Equilibrium is not staying constantly positive and avoiding the negative. It is allowing the negative to punctuate the positive, to give shape and definition to it by experiencing it and seeing its purpose. Equilibrium naturally occurs when we exist too long in one state, even a good state. We will inevitably experience opposition in life to give meaning and provide balance to our experience. Too often, we seek to avoid painful or uncomfortable experiences or emotions because we don't recognize their true purpose.

We are a culture addicted to distraction. We don't believe in self-nurture, not really. We are all for it if we can get it in a pill, or a product. We constantly purchase items marketed as being enriched with nourishing vitamins, herbs, or oils hoping they'll supply the missing element we need. We seek energy in 12-ounce metal cans and power in a snack bar. We are a counterfeit-seeking society. I have been successfully indoctrinated.

Only the epiphany accompanying this sunset has re-educated me. I have experienced an exquisite state to which no counterfeit could ever hold a candle. I have simply been too busy to allow space in my life for this condition to occur. How can something as simple as stillness and solitude nourish and nurture? How can the missing element of contentment suddenly emerge, and self-truth reveal its beauty when stimulated by these two simple tools? Could it be that I am always looking beyond the mark? Is the obvious too obvious? Is the simple too complex?

I lack faith. I don't trust that the simple, applied habitually, can deliver such deep results and rewards. I have become impatient with, and cynical about, simplicity. What I want is ease. Simplicity is not ease. In fact, simplicity takes diligent effort. I subconsciously trade simplicity for ease. But ease is like a weed that saps the root of life leaving its fruit scrawny, flavorless and with much to be desired. Ease leaves us believing that we are entitled to results without effort. We are deceived. On the other hand, simplicity requires work, but the rewards are immeasurable. Simplicity makes life meaningful. It creates space and invites movement. It is essential to contentment.

Self-truth cannot emerge in an over-crowded space. There simply isn't room. Nor can it be found in ease. There is no shortcut on the road to self-truth. Steps must be taken, emotions must be experienced, and thoughts must be allowed to surface in the process of self-revelation. Stillness and solitude are vital components of this process. They provide the atmosphere for healing and establishing equilibrium. The more we seek ease and deny simplicity, stillness and solitude, the more we feel a nagging sense there is something missing in life. And we don't even realize that what we're missing is ourselves.

The sun is lowering quickly and I will have to return to reality soon. I have experienced a breakthrough today in discovering a part of me I no longer knew existed. In a way, I have awakened. I'm aware there is something more to me and my world than pain and unhappiness, and I hold the key and the tools to change my life. I wish I could preserve this moment and access it at will. It would be so easy to feel peace and stillness near the ocean every day.

Remembering How to Breathe

Beautiful. Glorious. Breathtaking.

I'm sitting on the private patio of our condo. Birds are singing this afternoon as a warm wind kisses my skin. Palm trees peek over the masses of purple, orange and red Bougainvillea, star-shaped Plumeria and other exotic plants and shrubbery in my view. The faint whistle of the Sugar Cane Train floats across the breeze, humming gently in my ears. This place feels surreal.

I just woke from taking an afternoon nap, something I haven't done in years. Brett is still sleeping as I savor these few moments of solitude and silence. I feel a complete sense of relaxation, something I rarely feel, steeped as I am in my addiction to motion, busy to the core. Matt always comments on my inability to relax. I suppose he's right, but give me this environment consistently and I might actually master the art of relaxation!

A few moments before coming out onto the patio, I had the habitual urge to pull out my black binder stuffed with papers containing information on a current project waiting for me back home. This would be the perfect, quiet place to work. However, I stopped myself mid-motion as I leaned toward the bag where I had packed it. Instead, I listened to an inner voice of wisdom telling me this vacation is about filling the well, taking in and feeding the senses. It is a time for relishing the beauty, solitude and lushness of paradise. So here I sit, basking in the shaded comfort of the patio, pen in hand, writing, thinking, being.

I used to think a home in the country would be my ideal life, until I experienced this. This atmosphere feeds and supports me. The sea calms me, the vegetation fills my senses. This is a place of healing and nourishment. I feel so calm here, totally at one with this place. There is a stillness here I can't describe. I can picture myself living in a little house somewhere on the island. In my vision, I spend my days growing a garden year-round, meditating on the beach every morning at sunrise, soaking up the stillness, watching the evening sunset, finally learning to play my guitar, singing every day, taking care of my family, writing, teaching, and enjoying life.

I close my eyes and take a deep, long breath. Is this what it feels like to truly breathe? I can't remember. I haven't really breathed in so long. It comes so easily here on the patio, so naturally. I don't even have to try. With each exhale, anxiety and tension dissipate from my being, making room for beauty, peace and relaxation. It's truly a wonderful and long-neglected sensation.

We went to the beach this morning. The sound of the ocean was soothing and buffered the noise on the shore. I watched the hypnotic waves, like Earth's great lungs, breathing in and out, never ceasing, yet always changing. Sometimes strong, sometimes shallow, but always constant. It's a reassuring sound, reminding me again that life begins and abides with breath.

I tend to hold my breath when I am feeling anxious. It took several observations made by friends to bring this to my attention. No wonder I always feel so much tension in my shoulders! My muscles don't get enough oxygen! Still, I've done little to correct this problem. I know I need to change this unhealthy habit, but I've been too busy to address it. I don't have time to breath! How ridiculous is that?! Perhaps if I took the time to breath, I wouldn't feel so much stress in my life!

One thing I have observed in Maui is the pattern of thriving and flourishing. My son says the island is on steroids. The leaves are all big, bold and broad. The flowers are vibrant and prolific. Even the grass here has broad, flat blades that dwarf the varieties back home. The trees seem to be of two kinds, either slim towers reaching the sky or exotic canopies of lush vegetation with strangely crooked trunks and branches. Everything is so green, all shades, all vibrant. The combination of rainfall, humidity and sunshine offer perfect conditions for growth and allow these vivacious types of plant life to thrive in abundance, their true radiance revealed. Things can't help but grow here, me included. And growth begins with awareness. If I am not nourishing myself with something as essential and basic as full breaths of oxygen, how can I ever expect to flourish in my life? If I want a vibrant life, then I must find out what nourishes me on every level and apply it to my daily pattern of living.

Strange. As I write about the boldness of my surroundings, I look down on the patio floor and notice the tiniest ants I've ever seen! I guess it goes to show that there is balance and variety everywhere. I would expect the ants here to be enormous, and maybe there are species of huge ants on the island, but right here, right now, the ants on my patio are tiny! These small creatures remind me that I'm often enamored with the boldly beautiful and distracting things before my eyes, while neglecting to notice the small, seemingly unimportant things in my life, like breathing. Small things can be profound when we take the time to distinguish their importance from the glaringly large and seemingly obvious.

How often do I look only at those things either right in front of or around me? How often do I look beneath my feet, to my foundational elements, the very things that sustain me? At the invisible life below my view? My spirit? My emotions? How often do I look up toward the sky to be reminded that there is so much more than I can see? That I live in an endless universe?

Our lives are both large and small simultaneously. We see the life we choose to see. We choose the perspective from which to view it. We make ourselves both important and unimportant within our endless and tiny minds. We are a paradox and so is our world. Yet, within that opposition, we are unified and whole. We seek to make sense of wholeness and wholeness doesn't really make sense.

Wholeness is about balance, and I struggle with balance. Balance requires both the large and the small, careful attention to opposites. Balance is an elusive thing. I grasp for it, but I can't seem to hold on to it. It is the slipperiest substance on earth, so hard to obtain and so easy to lose. Because balance isn't one of those things you can store up for an off day. It must be earned anew with each sunrise. Balance is constantly shifting shape, wearing a new mask, changing color. It looks different every time I encounter it. Today's quest for balance is different than yesterday's quest because I'm not the same person I was yesterday. This isn't the same planet it was yesterday, and my resources are not exactly the same today as they were yesterday. And so it goes. I struggle on.

My tiny ants, like every other ant I have ever encountered, are so busy. They are on a mission, following a path to some invisible destination I can't see. Their activities unfortunately seem similar to my life back home, busy with no obvious purpose. But the ant's work is about physical survival and perpetuation of the colony. Mine is about numbing emotions with physical and mental activity. I am busy to perpetuate busyness, to distract myself and survive emotionally.

I suppose it comes back to breathing. As I breathe, I relax; as I relax, I allow. But I don't survive by allowing, I survive by controlling. Or at least that's what I believe. As humans, we tend to believe that if we can exercise a certain degree of control over our lives, we can block out the undesirable.

What is the quality of life we are living as we do so? I want to thrive, like the plants of the island. I want my life to be full of color and variety, full of beauty and peace. I want to flourish. But until I start breathing, until I start allowing and viewing my whole world, including the one within, rather than that which I just choose to see, I will not be able to thrive. I must remember and recover my ability to breathe, to breathe in life, to breathe in those elements that will help me flourish.

The Gift of Space

The first thing that struck me about the island was an incredible feeling of space.

Everywhere, space.

The endless ocean, the miles of uncluttered beaches, the two-lane roads lined with either farmland or island wilderness.

Space.

Even in the city, there is still this incredible feeling of space. It is amazing.

I currently live in the suburbs, in a valley that lies in the shadow of mountains. Houses and industrial buildings fill every available inch of view. My life is like my environment, crowded and busy. I frequently comment on the lack of space in my life. I have outgrown my home, outgrown my neighborhood, even my city. But the truth is that I have crowded my home with too much stuff, crowded my life with too many commitments that keep me from connecting with my neighbors and crowded my mind with too many beliefs that my place of residence is the source of my unhappiness. I have moved 18 times. What am I trying to find?

If I'm seeking space, it's the wrong kind. Escaping to something bigger or something newer is not escaping to space. Transferring my belongings to a bigger house, my schedule and habits to a new neighborhood or my attitudes to a new city only leads to buying more stuff, ignoring more people and blaming yet another city for my lack of fulfillment in life. No, the sense of space I crave is the sense of space that comes from selectivity, simplification and a life rhythm that allows me to feel joy and satisfaction. I am convinced that at the core we all crave this type of space because it's as vital as breathing in creating the perfect environment for a thriving life.

Upon entering this world, the very first act in which we engage is exhalation. If we don't rid ourselves of the products of the birth experience, we can't make room to receive the life experience. Clearing and emptying is essential to receiving and living. With each exhalation, we make room to receive oxygen. The larger we exhale, the greater the capacity to receive as we inhale. In other words, the more we let go, the more we can receive. This is true not only of our lungs, but of our lives.

This island teaches the great lesson of space, and I am completely flunking Space 101 in the school of life. I am failing to consciously create a life that breathes. I continually try to add more to my life, to do more, to be more, without ever clearing out the old to make room for the new.

Could it be that my self-esteem is attached to my productivity? Pair that with the need to silence my unpleasant emotions, and I repeatedly create a recipe for unhappiness. Of course, I don't see it that way. Rather, I tell myself that there are just so many good choices and it's hard to exclude myself from taking advantage of experiencing them all. I want it all. In return, I am fragmented and stretched too thin with ever-compounding and expanding problems.

Imagine if you could continue to take in oxygen without ever releasing any from your lungs. Soon your lungs would burst. Like a balloon with too much air inside of it, equilibrium will always be sought. We can only take on so much responsibility, so much pressure and fulfill so many expectations before we also burst, before equilibrium calls.

And it comes in many ways. Sometimes, it visits in the form of a nervous breakdown or detrimental health problems that force us to slow down. Other times, equilibrium comes quietly disguised as burn out, depression, or is masked in anxiety attacks and nightmares. These attempts are a subconscious call to address the expanding chaos that is building internally because of the way we are living externally. However, when equilibrium is dressed this way, we tend not to recognize it as the voice of internal wisdom forcing us to listen. We ply this unrecognized equilibrium with counterfeit solutions like drugs, distraction or addictive behaviors. I'm not saying that appropriate use of prescription or over-the-counter drugs, or healthy distractions aren't worthwhile. They are. But when plagued with undesirable ailments, if we would first recognize that some area of our life may be trying to equalize, we could then have the power to address issues that may be more emotionally based than physically based.

Space invites authenticity to emerge. At the core, we all long to live authentic lives, free from censure and shaming. We long to live our truth. Unfortunately, it's not culturally acceptable to live authentically and this creates a pain and longing we stifle in the name of conformity.

Conformity is the key to survival in society. Yet conformity denies the heart and leads to coping mechanisms required to deal with the void created by denial of the true self. We find ourselves stuck, walking through life like zombies, half-asleep, aching for that missing elusive something. We feel confused and frustrated because we don't even really know what it is that's missing. We blame relationships, jobs and financial matters when really what's missing is ourselves. We have crowded ourselves right out of the picture of our own lives in order to numb the pain of self-denial. The only way to welcome ourselves back into our lives is to create space.

How do we resolve the line between conformity and authenticity? Where is the balance? How do we live our truth while surviving in a world that rewards the wearing of masks? I suppose the solutions are as varied as the individuals seeking them. However, the denial of space in our lives perpetuates the problem. Space allows. Space is potential. Space provides room for one to create individual solutions to their particular battle between authenticity and conformity. Space is essential to knowing our innermost selves.

Peace is what we all seek, but so few of us know how to obtain it. Space is one of the prerequisites required for peace. As we are selective in our activities and commitments, our purchases, and in those things we hang onto, freedom and peace begin to emerge in our lives.

Space allows us to forgive. It is only in space that we come to terms with the discomfort in our lives, accept our role in that discomfort, forgive ourselves and others, and move on. To deny space is to deny true growth and progress. Denying space is an impediment to success, not outward, physical success (we all know unhappy people who are completely successful), but rather the success that brings true fulfillment, satisfaction and contentment.

The sea is vast and full. She is filled with life; she is filled with death. She hides secrets; she hides treasures. She is dark in many places and light in others. She is both deep and shallow. Her moods change, and yet she is constant. The sea embodies a life much like mine, but she is a master of the use of space. Every day at high tide, the sea ritualistically stretches her borders slightly, naturally growing, but in the process she accumulates debris. However, each day at low tide, she pulls back and discards that which is ready to be released. She lets go of that which she no longer needs. Whenever the sea heaves too far beyond her borders, devastation and destruction occur, delivering a potent lesson for those of us living too far beyond our means whether emotionally, physically, financially or otherwise.

The sea harbors only those things equipped to survive her rhythms. Whether in her womb or on her belly, she supports only those things that are uniquely fitted to the environment she offers. Likewise, as we take new activities, relationships, commitments and beliefs into our lives, we should be sure they are conducive to our well-being and environment, both internally and externally. We must discard what we don't need anymore, and we must do so consistently, habitually and with wisdom. Space is the great provider. It is the great canvas on which we design our lives. We alone fill the space we are given. We alone allow or deny space in our lives.

Space is a gift that is given to us without directions, and as a result we often misuse it. If we understand the principles behind it, we can create space easily. Selectivity breeds simplicity. Simplicity generates space. That's all. Great truths are seldom complex. However, it takes diligent awareness and concentrated effort to maintain space. That's the hard part. Maintaining space is high maintenance, but the rewards exceed the effort.

The sea is never stagnant. When we block the clearing process and simply accumulate, we are headed for trouble. We are headed toward the island of coping and denial, doomed to loneliness, dissatisfaction and confusion. I would much rather be like the sea, full of life, full of space, whole. Perhaps that's one of the reasons I feel such a deep longing for, and connection with the sea. She has mastered what I fail to manifest in my life, space.

Shifting Focus

I was hoping to be able to create a life vision here in Maui, but for most of my trip, I've felt lousy. Physically, this place is a high for me. My skin is more youthful and my countenance more vibrant. My entire body feels healthier here. The humidity and I agree. It's like I was born for this climate, but spiritually and emotionally, I have been in the dumps.

Matt is off scuba diving today so I take the kids on a mile-long walk along the beach to Whaler's Village where we pick up some souvenirs and enjoy berry-banana smoothies. Although the walk is hot and muggy, we take in the beauty of the neighboring resorts as we pass through them.

"Mom, this resort is so much prettier than ours," exclaims Chelsey, "Look at their swimming pools!"

"Yes, they are nice," I say, "but look how crowded they are. We practically have ours to ourselves."

"Yea, I guess you're right," she agrees.

The phrase the *grass is greener* comes to mind. How often do we look at what others have and wish we could enjoy the same thing? But I feel deeply satisfied and grateful for our condo because it feels more like a home than a hotel. And I love the privacy we enjoy at the pool and the beach because of the geography of our resort's location.

At Whaler's Village, we find a toy shop. I want to get Brett something for being so good on the long walk. He has a passion for soft stuffed animals, so we take him to the back of the store where the bottom display shelves are lined with baskets of stuffed animals.

He digs through each basket, testing the softness of each animal on his cheek until he finds a fluffy white seal. He looks at its face and squeals, "Cute! I love it!"

He sets it down on the shelf as he continues to explore other options. Each animal he picks up thereafter he compares with the seal. There is something about the face of the seal that keeps drawing him back. Though there are several seals, he knows which one is his. Each time he picks it up he looks it squarely in the face to make sure it's the right one. In the end, his choice remains the same.

I marvel at his ability to compare, contrast and choose so resolutely when I struggle daily to know what I want. I have so many choices, but then there was no shortage of stuffed toys for my son to choose from either. Perhaps the difference between our ability to choose resolutely lies in the fact that the two-year-old feels no pressure to choose in a particular way. With a toddler, you can encourage a certain selection but he knows what he wants and usually won't budge. You might succeed in distracting him for a moment or two but if the desired object remains within view, he is determined to have it. A two-year-old doesn't consider what he *should* choose. His criteria are few and simple. In this case, the look of the face and the feel of the fur.

I am so Martha-like, careful and troubled about so many things. I am everybody's rock and if I crumble, so do they. At least that's what I believe. That's a lot of pressure. I am tired of always feeling everybody's expectations on my back. I am tired of my own expectations. How do you know what you want if you've never experienced anything other than "should"? Babies have no "shoulds" and are able to pick their heart's desire.

What if I shed my shoulds? What if I let go of expectations and judgments in my mind? Like my little toddler running around in his diaper, I want to be free of complexity, burden, judgment and inhibition. I want to stand in my true nature. I've forgotten what that feels like.

We talk about finding ourselves. We crave liberation, not from *who* we are, but *how* we are. How we are is safe, but how we are is also stifling and draining. So how do you break down *how* you are and reveal *who* you are? And if, like me, you begin to sense *who* you are and begin to shed *how* you are, how do you expand that? And how do you maintain that when you have to go back to, or exist in, an environment that supports *how* you are? Do you have to abandon your current life to "find" yourself?

That's certainly not what I want and I don't really think it's the answer. I think we *think* that is the answer. Finding yourself means discovering that life is a process, figuring out where you are in that process, redefining yourself, and working with what you have to build what you want. It requires changes, but not necessarily total renovation. Or does it?

I have pretty much questioned everything while here in Maui. My soul has erupted with explosions of "What do I want?! Who am I?! And how do I change my life?!" I have come face to face with many ugly questions about my life and the options of perceived *freedom* that could change things for me.

Though I don't have all the answers right now, I know that I don't just want change. I want meaningful change. So I postpone making any decisions for now. I believe that when we sit with our choices for awhile, the truth rises. When we refrain from drastic or immediate action in the moment of emotion, we rise above our feelings and the still, perfect truth emerges with time. Time will unlock the mystery; time will bring the answers I seek. Now the challenge becomes cultivating the patience to wait for that revelation.

Revelation requires surrender, being open to receiving the truth however it manifests. Everyone wants to feel like they have control over their life and I am no exception. But I have become so desperate for clarity that finally I'm willing to release that need for control, the need to know and understand everything right now. It requires faith in God, faith in myself, faith in the world around me and in the people I love.

Faith can be a scary tool to wield, but it is a powerful tool. How long do I wait to exercise faith until there seems to be no other option? Can it even be called faith if I am acting out of desperation? In its simplest form, faith is movement, action. If I am seeking, and that seeking is voluntary, I *must* be exercising faith. Desperation is simply the motive, or impetus to that movement, that faith.

I must acquire voluntary faith if I want powerful answers, powerful change. As long as I fear the revelation that comes through exercising faith, my answers will remain weak and unclear. They will only be parts of the truth. I will only allow my conscious mind to connect to the answers that I am ready to receive. Powerful faith means that I will surrender to the truth regardless of what it reveals or what it may ask of me. And that can be scary, even stunt the growth of faith.

Every time I act without knowing the outcome, but hoping for the best, I exercise faith. Every time I get disappointed when my hopes don't manifest according to my faith, I have the opportunity to exercise surrender. Faith and surrender are partners.

Another way to look at faith is through desire. When we desire we seek, or work to acquire. That is faith. When we surrender, we render our hearts to the truth. Faith, along with love, is the greatest power on earth. It moves me to act, to dream, to become, to change, and to receive, as does love. As a motivator, love is incredibly powerful. Faith motivated by love heals. Loving myself enough to act in accordance with the truth inside my heart about who I am, what I am meant to become, and what I can give to this world is rare gift indeed.

We finally return to our condo dripping with sweat. I bathe Brett and he falls instantly asleep on the bed. I pull off my sticky clothes, shower and put on something light to cool off in. I feel different. It is almost as if in putting on these new clothes, I have somehow put on a newer, lighter outlook as well.

The last few days have been strange, but equilibrium has finally come calling with a gracious gift—a turning of the tide, some reprieve, some balance from the darkness I've been feeling. Far too often, we react rashly in an effort to rid ourselves of the painful feelings we may be experiencing in life. I have been forced to sit with my feelings. I may not have done it gracefully, but I have allowed myself to look at the wounded and undesirable parts of my life. I have allowed myself to feel the irrational feelings that have surfaced. I didn't act, I just felt, uncomfortable as it was, and I have been taught unforgettable lessons in the process.

By acknowledging that it's okay to feel how I feel, by accepting that this is where I am right now, my current truth, I've been working an unseen miracle in my life. I have been freeing myself and I didn't even realize it. Until we acknowledge and accept the truth as it is, we cannot be free of that truth, nor can we create a new truth.

Brett is sleeping next to me as I write in my journal, exhausted from our two-mile trek. He is snuggling with his new stuffed seal, the prize for being dragged through the heat and sun. He is beautiful. He threw a tantrum when we got to Whaler's Village. He was hot and tired and had sand in his shoes. I offered him a smoothie but he wouldn't have it. He needed to cry out his frustrations, so we went outside the smoothie shop and he screamed. Toddlers have such wisdom. They feel what they feel and they cry about it. They don't try to stifle it, or run from it. Once they cry, they let it go and move on. They instinctively know how to work through their emotions in a healthy way. Social conditioning has taught us otherwise.

As he cried, I calmly waited. When he was finished, he climbed up next to me on a chair. I handed him the smoothie, he took a nice long drink, looked up at me with his deep brown eyes and said with a breathless sigh, "Thank you, Mommy."

How sweet is that?

It was a beautiful moment, a lesson and a reminder that release brings reprieve.

Observing Beauty

I have thought much about beauty since arriving in Maui. I have asked myself repeatedly: What is beauty? What makes something beautiful? Is it the exoticness of the experience that creates it? Exotic is simply a way to label something that's different from the norm. It's definitely different here. Back home, conformity to expectation is the norm for beauty. Here, the whole island screams of originality and boldness. Why is originality and boldness of expression considered desirable and beautiful in nature? Why not in humans? When it comes to people, we have such a narrow definition of what is beautiful. Aren't we all exotic in some way? Why do we value variety in nature and not in people? We are called individuals for a reason—because we are each unique and different. Isn't that beautiful?

Beauty is not perfection. That's too narrow and exclusive a definition. As I walk through the resort parks and along the beach, I notice an emerging pattern. Although my surroundings are well manicured and well cared for, they are not "perfect" in the sense of the word as we usually define it. Proof of the cycles of nature is on the ground in the form of fallen Plumeria flowers and palm pods. But as the trees shed their flowers, signifying the end of a cycle, they simultaneously sprinkle joy at my feet.

Beauty.

At the beach I discover space, also a form of beauty. The beach is the epitome of simplicity. Simplicity is beauty.

On the road to Hana, I discover another kind of beauty, not the open space I find near the ocean. On the contrary, the road is lush and proliferated with trees, shrubs and plants in all varieties. It is the beauty of fullness that I find; the beauty of maturity. The plants compliment the landscape, working together to create a tropical paradise. They support one another in building a picture of life flourishing. They balance the open space that is so prevalent on the island.

Beauty.

Truth also is beautiful. As I embrace my truth and discover that my feelings are not who I am, but only an expression of my experiences, I find beauty. Truth is always beautiful, though not always comfortable. Truth brings freedom.

Every time I fall short of my expectations, there is still beauty to be found in the reaching. Recognizing the constant manifestations of beauty in life is a habit that must be cultivated. Too often, we focus on the way we fall short of beauty, rather than how we fulfill beauty in our lives. I have spent far too many years of my life absolutely believing that I was completely excluded from any form or manifestation of beauty in my life. But it simply isn't true. The island has blessed me with eyes to see.

Beauty is encompassed in anything that touches the heart, anything that moves us toward a sense of love, stillness, serenity and joy. Much here has moved me to recognize beauty. But because I have spent so much time focusing on what I lack, at first I failed to see how abundant beauty really is in my life.

Beauty is a process, not a destination. Beauty is defined by the shadows of pain that draw its loveliness forth. Like any great piece of artwork, both darkness and light are required for the image to emerge on the canvas. Only through contrast can beauty be identified.

It is evening now. Matt and I drive to Front Street and share a waffle bowl full of ice cream. We eat it while sitting on a stone wall, the ocean breaking just a few feet below and behind us, the fingernail moon hanging somewhat transparently in the dusky sky.

We chat a bit about how careful we've become over the years in certain ways and how that trait has limited us in many aspects of our lives. We talk of other less heavy things. The conversation is good. The company is good, and welcome. On our way back to the car, we stop in an art gallery to view some of the unusual and eye-catching works inside. There are many beautiful paintings, so many different styles, so many perspectives of beauty, all valuable, all meaningful.

On the ride home, we talk about the possibility of parasailing the next day and comment on tattoos. I have never considered getting a tattoo, and determined that I never would, but if that were something I pursued, I knew exactly what it would be. A symbol of transformation, strength born in struggle, beauty and freedom (the lessons I've learned in Maui), I would choose a butterfly.

Fish Back in Water

We have the pool all to ourselves this morning. Matt and the kids are splashing merrily in the water as I sit at the side of the pool. I haven't swum with my head in the water in over fifteen years. Why? As a teenager, one of my guy friends told me I looked funny when I was wet. He planted a seed that eventually sprouted and grew into a beanstalk of gigantic proportions when Matt gave me *The List* (all the things he disliked about me) early in our marriage. After that, I never got back in the water above my waist again. It wasn't a conscious decision. I just felt the sting of thoughtless remarks and somehow associated water with pain. To avoid any more pain, I simply avoided anything that might render me more frightful to look at, like swimming.

To avoid swimming throughout the years, I've used the excuse that I hate the coldness of the water. This is true. I really do hate the cold, but this excuse became my crutch, a way to avoid potential emotional pain. How often do I claim dislike of a particular activity without even questioning the origin of that dislike?

From the pool, Matt suddenly hands me his snorkel gear and suggests that I learn how to use it before going into the ocean. I hadn't planned on snorkeling, using Brett as an excuse.

As a child, I swam almost every day with my friends. I was a little fish. I loved it. But having carried my negative beliefs, and having avoided swimming for so long, I resist his suggestion. I look around the pool, we are the only people in it. I put on the gear and down into the water I go. Something amazing happens. I had thrown myself out of the water years ago and had been drying out ever since. Now, as I sink into the heated pool, kicking the fins behind me and gliding through the water, I feel a freedom wash through my entire body. A part of me that had been long silenced is awakened. I feel weightless, not just because the water is buoying me up, but because I have finally broken through a long-honored mental, emotional and physical limitation. Such a simple act, and yet so healing.

In the afternoon, I find myself standing with my feet in the wet sand on the shoreline, the ocean waves breaking around my ankles. It is cold. Slowly I inch my way into the waves, directing empty threats at Kale and Chelsey who are attempting to speed my progress along by splashing me. Why am I resisting the experience in front of me? Didn't I have a breakthrough at the pool earlier? No. To truly overcome this block, I must consistently take every opportunity that presents itself to me to reclaim the freedom and joy of swimming. I've got to break down any and every barrier associated with the activity. I might never have another chance to swim in the oceans of Maui. I know that I need to jump in, but I'm finding it difficult. Old patterns die hard. I struggle for a moment and then dive into the water head first. It is still cold, really cold. It takes longer to get used to than I would like, but once I adjust, it feels wonderful.

It takes a few minutes to get my gear properly situated and to get used to breathing solely through my mouth, but once I get the hang of it, I find I love snorkeling! I float along on the salt sea weightlessly. There is a completely different world under the ocean and it's amazing! The water is so clear here, kind of like how life becomes once we remove resistance and dive beneath the surface of our physical and emotional world.

In dream interpretation, water is a symbol for the unconscious mind. There is so much swimming around in the unconscious that we will not discover unless we dive in and explore.

While snorkeling, I find it natural to look at what is directly beneath and around me. But as I look out into the deep, less visible waters, and up at the surface, I discover more surprises. At the surface, I notice all kinds of little silver Needlefish. Blending in with the water, they are almost transparent. As I strain my eyes out to sea, I observe massive schools of fish, moving like patches of shadow through the deep. There is so much to see in the ocean that might otherwise be missed if you're not fully searching your surroundings.

Along the reef, schools of Convict Tang pick at algae, and cleverly camouflaged Black Crabs crawl along the black rocks. I have something in common with the Needlefish and Black Crabs. They are masters of disguise and so am I. Not only for the sake of survival that conformity affords, but also for the emotional safety it lends, I frequently and unconsciously try to blend in. To stand out from the crowd is dangerous because it puts one at risk of rejection, ridicule, and validates that there is something wrong, something lacking. To stand out from the crowd is to become a target for criticism, and who needs that?

So I creep along in my life, like these little creatures, safe, but limited. Yet, as I study them, I see them for what they are, not part of the landscape, blended and unremarkable, but individual and beautiful creatures with purpose. Beauty emerges from conscious observance. My beauty is only realized as I see my purpose, my individuality and my remarkableness. Though I have yet to really discover these things. However, unlike my new saltwater friends, I'm not required to stay in the background hiding. I can overcome those limitations, just as I have overcome my "dislike" of swimming. But will I?

When I first began snorkeling, I panicked a few times. Breathing only through my mouth, and not having swum in so long, I was unsure of my abilities, but gradually I became more comfortable. Moving from fear and dislike into comfort and joy is a process that emerges only at the rate the participant allows. In other words, I control the rate of change in my life. I will only allow what I am ready to experience and no more. If I was not ready to surrender my trust to the fact that my snorkeling equipment would support my snorkeling activities, I would experience additional resistance to the activity and my ability to move from fear to joyful experience would be slowed, or might never occur. I cannot force the rate of allowance. It must happen naturally. I was ready to let go of my long-standing anti-swimming attitude, and recognized that it no longer served me. I also recognize that my outdated attitude had the potential to deprive me of a possible once-in-a-lifetime opportunity of snorkeling in these glorious waters. The speed of my recovery was in direct relation to my readiness to let go of old beliefs and my willingness to exercise faith that the experience would benefit me and be worthwhile. I choose willingness and faith. I choose the rate of change I experience in this moment, but only because I am at a point where I am ready for it.

I drift on the water and am suddenly aware that this moment will soon end. I take a mental picture of it so that I can remember it always. I savor the liberating, floating sensation of the water surrounding me and I am grateful. It's strange. I have never lived from such a place of awareness and detachment. From a place where I am aware and grateful even in the moment, that I am experiencing the gift. To define this experience as a gift is a gift in itself. I have always lived from a place of reminiscence and being grateful *after* something has occurred. I am learning to be present and give thanks in every moment as I experience it. This ability gives even more meaning to the moment and fills me with awe.

By late afternoon the sky has turned gray. The wind is blowing pretty hard, but I am ready to test even more limits. My rebirth into the love of water has opened my mind and I am ready to take more risks, albeit calculated risks. Matt and I are standing on the beach of the neighboring resort staring out at the ocean, waiting for the little boat that will take us out to a parasailing adventure. We are debating whether to go with 500 or 1,200 feet of line. He leaves the final choice up to me. After a few minutes of internal debate, I decide on the longer line and even splurge for the photo package.

The water is really choppy, making it hard to stay balanced as we transfer ourselves from the little boat onto the parasailing craft. All of the couples on board are doing tandem rides. We are second in line. My stomach churns with excitement as we step out onto the platform and get buckled into our straps. I'm not even nervous.

The attendant hooks the parachute to our leg-straps and a few seconds later the boat speeds out from beneath us and we fly into the air. It's exhilarating. We are floating away from the boat, from the earth, from the cares of life. We climb higher and higher, the air grows increasingly more silent with every foot of line released. I am not afraid. I feel like a child sitting in a giant swing suspended in the sky, totally carefree and joyful. It feels like a dream.

Except for an occasional comment, Matt and I don't speak. Some moments don't require words. In this instant, we were as free as birds, flying between the clouds, soaring without a care. This is a sacred moment, and I know it. I am grateful to know it. Recognizing sacred moments brings meaning to life. It allows us to cherish experience. And some experiences only happen once.

The driver begins to reel us back in. As we approach the craft, he lowers us down into the water for a toe touch and then raises us back up again for another minute. Before I know it, we are back on the platform and our ride is over. I'm a little sad that it's come and gone so quickly.

Overcome by fear, the third couple on the boat decides not to take the ride. I am sad for them. I know what they are missing. On many occasions, fear prevents joy. I've discovered that although I love new experiences, I make very little room in my life for them. After today, I'm determined to change that.

Gentle Lessons

The sea is calm tonight. The air is warmer than the last few nights at this hour. I come out here every night, alone. It has become my ritual. I have come to love this sacred time on my rock near the ocean. Sometimes I sit on the sand, like tonight. It doesn't matter. I embrace the solitude and relish in it.

The waves come in gently tonight, almost delicately, softly lapping at the rocks, no great emotion or fervor, just quiet and caressing. The sea speaks of the sweet release that comes as one begins to shed the unnecessary, the encumbered, the constricting. Whispering to my heart, she sends blessings that encourage me to keep peeling back the layers. I feel the need to uncover the truth until I am completely bare, until the skin of my soul stands naked, flaws and all. Until I no longer recoil, but embrace; until I no longer hide but seek; until I no longer hate but love; until I no longer sleep but am fully awake, alive and vital.

I watch the sunset for awhile. As always, it is different tonight. As the sun sinks toward the horizon, it becomes a thin, giant red disk slipping in and out of the clouds between slots in the sky.

Beautiful.

I'm finding that when I'm drawn to something, it's because it holds a message for my soul. There is a quality in the place, thing, or experience before me that nourishes me in some way. The sea is one of those things that draws me in. The sunset is another. The beauty of nature provides instant therapy to the soul. It's always available and endless in variety. No need to call ahead. Just come as you are in your moment of need. Mother Nature will calm you, fill you and bless you with her bounteous beauty and endless secrets. You just have to be still of mind in order to unlock the messages hidden on her subtle breath. You have to desire to receive, and then allow.

To my left are the black rocks, on top of which is built a concrete platform that stretches out to the waters, a lookout of sorts. It is enclosed with a chain-link fence. A sign posted on the fence says Keep Out, but people are always out there fishing and looking at the ocean. In fact, the fence is even peeled back for easy access to the platform.

There is a couple up there now, kissing and watching the sunset. I had considered visiting the platform myself, just before they came, but refrained because of the warning sign on the fence. I always obey the signs. I never take risks and life is passing me by! Funny, as soon as I saw them go through the fence, I felt I like I had permission to go there myself, but it was too late, they were already there.

I'm always looking for permission for my actions. I suppose it comes from being censured for so many years in so many ways. It's a long-held belief from the past. *You better be careful in your decision and actions or it will bring you pain.* This belief no longer serves me. I see it now as a thorn in my side, stealing potential joys from manifesting in my life. I'm determined to experience a life of conscious joy. I am choosing to see the beauty of the moments as they appear in my life. I am choosing to challenge my long-held, joy-sucking, "safe" beliefs. I am choosing to take calculated risks, to experience life more fully.

The sun has gone down; dusk has arrived. I will have to return to the condo soon, and to my crabby toddler who is restless, over-stimulated and missing his home. To soothe him, I'll scoop him up into my arms and wrap his tiny frame in a big hug, my heart filled with gratitude for the opportunity to be his mother.

Today, I am filled with gratitude for what is. What a contrast from the first few days of my trip. As I choose the way I perceive my life in each moment, I am released from the bondage of unconscious perception, of experiencing my life in a state of powerlessness. Instead of reacting to the moment in a victimized or habitual way, I experience freedom. Funny how many emotions and themes one can cycle through in a short period of time.

Like the ocean waves, life is not static. It is a cycle, a process, a repetition of a few basic lessons played out in various forms and patterns over and over again until we finally learn from them what we need to learn on a conscious level. The lessons, like the waves, rise up and sometimes swell, but we often don't notice what they are trying to teach us.

Today, the sea gently encourages me to embrace life. It is a lesson that has been knocking on my door for years, but I have failed to answer it until the ocean whispered it to my heart and I was finally ready to listen.

I marvel at life. I cycle from stillness to chaos to awakening to conscious movement. And I will cycle back again, just as I should, through the never-ending circle of life, learning and growing, through seasons and change.

Life is not linear. When it becomes linear, when it fails to vary, it's an indication that we are stagnant. I have grown tired of stagnation. I will keep this image of the gentle sea in my mind. I will heed her lesson that life is ever-changing and in those changes, joy is found. Balance between stillness and movement, the journey and the destination, is what life is all about.

Ebb and Flow

Today is our last full day and night in Maui. The kids are homesick and can't wait to return. They miss their belongings, their familiar beds and their friends. Matt and I have no desire to return to our lifestyle at home. Perhaps after six months we might, but a week just isn't enough. As I prepare myself mentally to return, I am confronted with the question of how to create more space in my life at home? *How can I take the rhythm of the island back with me?* I don't know if I can.

Time away from home does one of two things. It either makes you totally appreciate where you are and what you have, or it brings home the stark realization that you are not really living, that you are failing to embrace a life of consistent meaning. If something is missing from life then the trick becomes pinpointing exactly how to incorporate the missing elements into the mix and create a new existence.

I recognize that I attach certain feelings and desires to Maui that may only exist because of the fact that I am on vacation. The easy or counterfeit solution would be to just move here. But if I transfer my home life to Maui, it will eventually feel as stale as it does back home because it's simply a physical transfer, not a holistic change. No, changes must be made at a deeper level. Transfer does not equal transformation. Transfer is easy. Transformation requires work. It is the shedding of comfort zones and the shifting of the shape of one's life. Like a butterfly, I must work hard to break free from the chrysalis of protection I've built around myself. Only after the hard work of pushing beyond limits can I hope to feel the soaring experience of freedom and realize the true form I am meant to assume.

The afternoon wears on as I busy myself doing laundry and packing. I finally get Brett to nap. It's already 3:30 in the afternoon and I have a splitting headache that won't go away. I should probably take a nap, but I want to spend a few minutes on the patio writing because I know it will be the last time I get to do so. We have to check out of our condo by 11:00o'clock tomorrow morning. I feel sad. I am not ready to leave. I love it here. I will miss the warmth of the humid breeze cooling my skin when the sun gets too hot. I will miss the reminder that life flourishes in the right conditions. I will miss the textures, the greenery, the contrasting colors of vivid flowers, the banana plants outside my door, the quiet, the ocean, the birds, and the very air that hushes the noise so prevalent back home. I will miss the space!

Evening comes and I walk down to the beach. I want to spend this last sunset on the lookout and experience what I passed up the other night out of fear. As I approach the sand, I can see that the lookout is full of fishermen. I should have taken the chance when I had it the other night. Once lost, some opportunities are gone forever. It's so disheartening to know you've missed a chance that will never come again.

The beach is almost completely empty tonight. Only a handful of people are scattered along the shores and they are far away from me. I soak up the moment as I walk, the dry, cool sand pushing up between my toes. A gentle breeze wraps around me, holding me in a goodbye hug. I am having a hard time knowing this may be the last time I ever get to walk along this beach.

Sunsets represent the end of a cycle. How symbolic. Not only is it the end of my vacation, but maybe the reason I've been so drawn to the beach at sunset is because I've sensed closure approaching in my own life. I feel the need to discard those things that no longer serve me, to say good-bye to an era of limitation.

I sit on the sand for a long time, quiet and still. I feel solemn and peaceful, sad and grateful, moved and happy all at the same time. I thank God for the gift of Maui, for the gift of the sea, for the gifts I discovered while here. I think again of the butterfly. My life has been like that caterpillar, gorging away, stuffing myself with so many meaningless distractions, never stopping to gauge how it's affecting me. Yet, all this has prepared me for profound change. A chrysalis has formed around me over the years and Maui is the trigger that has cracked that chrysalis. The hard work of breaking free lies ahead of me, but one day I will fly free. I will look back on the struggles of my life and wonder why I waited so long to change.

An End and a Beginning

Our flight got pushed back! It doesn't leave until 9:00 o'clock tonight. Normally, that would be terribly inconvenient, but Matt called the condo owner and we can stay until 6 tonight instead of having to check out by 11 as formerly agreed. What luck that no one is checking in for two days! I can't imagine trying to kill ten hours with a two-year-old and no place to nap, eat or play!

An extra day at the beach!

God is good.

We grab our gear and hit the path to the ocean. I splash into the water without hesitation, ready to snorkel. There are even more fish near the reef today than when I snorkeled a few days ago. I swim around easily, confidently. The water feels warmer today. As I float along, I feel both wonder and sadness. The fish are delightful, but this final swim is my goodbye. I don't want to get out of the water. I hate goodbyes. I take my time, literally dragging my fins, but finally get out and pass them to Matt.

As I stand on the shores, my feet sinking into the warm sand, I notice that the lookout from where I thought I would never get to view the ocean is empty. I climb up the black rocks as quickly as I can and scramble up to the platform. The jagged rocks hurt my bare feet, but I don't care. I feel like I've received a second chance, a sweet mercy on a tiny desire of my heart that really served no one but me. It seems so trivial and yet I need to stand here, to see the ocean from a different perspective, to do the thing I wanted to do, but didn't because of fear.

Yesterday, it seemed like it would never happen for me, but today the impossible has become possible. I stand where I thought I would never stand and I am filled with joy. Suddenly I am given a rare gift. As I look down into the deep blue water, a huge sea turtle swims up to the surface directly below me and pokes his head out. He looks up at me and our eyes meet for a moment. His serene face, full of wisdom and experience won through the struggles of life, tells me that gifts are everywhere, that second chances are sacred experiences, not to be wasted or taken advantage of.

As the turtle dives back into the water, I rush as quickly as I can back to the beach. I'm excited to share this rare experience with my family, especially Matt. When he went diving the other day he hoped to see a sea turtle, but the opportunity never presented itself. I hand him the snorkel gear as I tell him of my discovery and he dashes out into the water, swimming out around the rock as fast as he can. He is gone for quite awhile. I'm saddened because I fear he's missed the opportunity to see the turtle, but eventually he comes back smiling. Not only did he see it, but they swam together for a few moments. This experience instantly reminds me of how animals love Matt.

At the zoo one day, an elephant reached its trunk out and touched Matt's hand as he extended it. He didn't even have any food in his hand! Another time, a giraffe leaned its head down and let Matt pet it as he fed it a branch. Now, a turtle in the Pacific Ocean has let him share a swim. It makes me wonder what these animals see in him that engenders their trust so easily. Perhaps they see what I see, his core goodness. We all have it, though I am convinced that certain circumstances bring out the light and goodness within us more readily than others. This was one of those circumstances for Matt.

Though I didn't see it at first, Maui has been one of those circumstances for me. It's been pulling me into the light more than I have been in a long time. It is pulling me home to myself.

What will happen when I return to my physical home? I don't know, but I am resolved not to let the knowledge that I have received on the island go to waste. Maui has been a reminder to me that after the trial comes the blessing. To be stripped of pretense, pride, masks and perceptions, to stand naked before oneself, to behold one's flaws long enough to get past the discomfort and annoyance is to receive a gift. It is the beginning of the journey toward personal transformation. It is the journey toward gaining wings.

As we gather our things, shaking the sand from them, I take one long last look at the ocean, my ocean, for she belongs to whomever will claim her and receive the gifts she has to offer. I breathe deeply and feel gratitude wash over me for what has transpired during this short trip. I am not the same person I was a week ago.

I didn't come on vacation to soul search or analyze my life, but that's what happened. And I sense that the journey has only just begun.

Book IV

A Crown and Wings

"After a while you learn the subtle difference between holding a hand and chaining a soul, and you learn that love doesn't mean leaning and company doesn't mean security...You begin to accept your defeats with your head up and your eyes open, with the grace of an adult, not the grief of a child...So, you plant your own garden and decorate your own soul, instead of waiting for someone to bring you flowers. And you learn that you really can endure... that you really are strong, and you really do have worth."

~Veronica A. Shoffstall

White Flag

As the months fly by, it's amazing how pain can become a normal part of life. In many important ways, the pageant and my trip to Maui have made me stronger and less tolerant of disrespectful behavior, chaos and tension. Yet that same strength has ironically created more tension, chaos and a greater unhappiness in my life.

I continue to work with great diligence on myself, knowing I cannot change others. The more I heal, the more I understand just how much I have betrayed myself by trying to be "perfect", by silently begging for acceptance and approval. I can no longer play that role, no matter how hard the path of self-reclamation becomes. I sense difficult choices on the horizon and I'm not sure I have the strength to make them.

When I was making dinner a few minutes ago, the kids and their dad started arguing. I left the room.

Lying on my bed, the deep brown eyes of my sweet toddler, Brett, peak over the edge of the mattress, "I want to lay by you, Mommy," he says as he climbs up next to me. A look of concern crosses his tiny face, "What happened to you, Mommy?"

"Nothing, I'm just sad," I say as I stroke his smooth cheek.

"What happened to you?" He asks again. "Dad?"

How can a three-year-old understand so much? I didn't say anything about his dad. I didn't even engage in the argument that was going on in the next room, and still he picks up on the source of my sorrow.

We snuggle together for awhile and he falls asleep next to me. He is so beautiful. He doesn't deserve to grow up in a house full of contention.

A few weeks ago, Matt and I had a discussion. He tried to convince me to see the error of my ways. He told me I should give up my dreams and goals and just be happy being a mom. I am happy being a mom. I've been a stay-at-home mom for our entire 18 -year marriage. I even spent 14 of those years homeschooling my kids. I love being a mom more than anything! But over the years, I've expressed my desire to pursue some of my dreams, in addition to being a mom. Isn't it okay to want good things? To develop myself? To express myself? To serve others outside the family sphere too? Isn't it a wonderful example for my children to see me chase my dreams, learn new things and accomplish goals?

I think so.

The discussion quickly turned toward divorce and I knew there was much more behind his comments than simple frustration with my aspirations. I have never sacrificed the needs of my family for the sake of my dreams and we both knew it.

I finally realized the real issue. His request was an ultimatum of sorts, *either my spirit or our marriage*. He was asking me to stop trying to heal, to just be the version of me he'd become familiar with, so he could feel secure within himself. For most of our marriage, he had known me as a weak and insecure person and now I was becoming strong and independent. He could feel it. Change is threatening to those around us who are used to, and comfortable with, our weaknesses and habitual behaviors.

Ever since that conversation, I have been struggling. I can feel divorce looming in the future like an impending death, and it scares me. So I struggle and I fight it. One side of me wants desperately to keep my family together, to heal this broken relationship with Matt. The other side absolutely requires that I respect myself and claim ownership of my spirit. The battle feels like it's over whom I love more, me or my spouse. Can't I love both? Why does it feel like an either-or choice?

A heavy sigh escapes my lips. I am tired of fighting. I don't see how I can leave anyway. I have no college education. I have no work experience. How would I take care of myself and my children? I feel like I have no choice but to stay. I feel like the decision already has been made for me. I feel defeated. Happiness is for other people. I raise a metaphorical white flag. It still feels easier to sacrifice myself than to lose my marriage, my comfort and my security.

A few days later, I settle into a compromise with Matt. I agree to become even more diligent and concerned at home if he will make specific commitments in return. I work to fulfill my end of the bargain daily, but have yet to see him make an effort on his commitments.

We discuss my observations and he claims that he *can't* do what we agreed upon. I have surrendered myself to make this work, and for what? A one-sided effort? His peace and comfort at the expense of my own? Yes, I may have shelter, food, clothing and my family all under one roof, but in exchange, I get a daily helping of self-betrayal, anxiety and unhappiness. In essence, I have chosen prison in exchange for physical security. And I know that the prison of a life without love, respect and happiness will ultimately kill me. I can feel my strength slipping away.

The Lines We Draw

A friend of mine wants to give a song (that I invited him to co-write with me) to a local band, but I don't want to. Sure it could mean some royalties, but I intended this song for an established star; I want to pitch this song in Nashville. My dream is to have Rascal Flatts sing it, not a local band, at least not until we have given Nashville a real shot. I've been struggling with his request for a few hours now and I'm puzzled by the intensity of my resistance and the pressure I feel, even though my friend is not pressuring me at all.

After much introspection, I locate the source of the pressure. It's inside of me. Pressure always comes from within as a response to external stimuli that we are resisting for internal reasons.

I'm now aware of several insights as I have pondered this, but most prominent is a pattern of surrender in my life. I feel like I'm always surrendering. Recent conversations in my marriage have punctuated this fact clearly. To keep the peace, I have always been the more submissive partner. Again and again, I have constantly compromised myself, giving up my wants, needs and wishes for others. I believe I can't have the things that will truly make me happy so I sacrifice, sacrifice, and sacrifice some more.

I don't respect or love myself enough to hold my ground. I don't honor myself. I don't know how to be "selfish" in a healthy way, or disappoint people. I'm already such a disappointment. If the person who is supposed to love me more than anyone doesn't love me, and criticizes me even when I give my best, then how will anybody else ever love, or even like me? Especially if I disagree with them?!

The first great commandment of Christianity is to love God, and then to love your neighbor *as yourself*! I am commanded to love myself, but I fail to do so and am miserable because of it. Sometimes I even blame God for my suffering, telling myself that he wants me to be humble and broken, but it isn't God that constantly asks me to surrender. From time to time, He may ask it of me, but not constantly. Rather, it's my false belief in the lie masquerading as truth in my brain that wants me to surrender so that I can feel loss and pain and, oddly enough, peace in the comfort of my discomfort. It is equilibrium of a different kind. It's the equilibrium of familiarity. My body, mind and emotions rush to that familiar plane of surrender and pain. It is what I know. But it is not what I want.

These struggles, these lines I have drawn, have got to go. So, for the first time in a long time, I stand my ground. I tell my friend that I do not want to go with the opportunity presented by the local band using our song. Surprisingly, he respects my decision. And even more surprising, we are still friends. What a strange phenomenon! Is this what healthy relationships are like? Is this what it's like to have a real friend? Is this what it's like to be emotionally healthy?

A few days later, life presents another opportunity that tests my new awareness about the lie that I must always surrender. I immediately begin to feel resistance, but this time I recognize it and I ask myself: what do I *really* want? I think. I decide. I follow through. And I continue down the path of self-healing and self-love.

Gone

I am at my mom's house tonight. Matt and I have decided to get a divorce. I am so numb. Red-faced and sobbing, I feel anguish and anger and everything in between rushing through me. All I can do is lie here on the guest bed and cry. My stomach churns with nausea. This is my family, and I am losing the most precious thing in my life. As I grieve, wretchedness is my only embrace tonight. I have failed, and in the most important endeavor I have ever undertaken—my marriage.

Tears flow.

Around this time last year, Matt and I took a pretty huge and devastating blow to our marriage. He told me that those events caused him to realize that he really did love me, but after just a few weeks of trying to change, things started going even more downhill. Why is that?

I think my biggest mistake after last year's incident was denial. I mentally forgave, but didn't process or cope with the situation at a heart level. I just kept telling myself I was fine, but I wasn't. We moved forward, broken and weak, becoming more deformed with time, and less able to handle each subsequent blow delivered to our already fragile relationship.

I stare at the ceiling, wiping the wetness from my cheeks. I understand the consequences of this decision. I have been clinging to the familiar. I don't want divorce, but I don't have the energy to constantly protect this newly planted seed of self-love in my heart that I know will shrivel amidst the constant cloud of darkness and adversarial weeds of contention that threaten to choke and destroy it. Can't I just be who I am without having to always justify that I am worthy of existence?

We are a clash of titanic proportions, Matt and I. Harmonious as oil and water, we can't get along. We are not necessarily wrong in who we are, we are just wrong together.

Our marriage has suffered a slow and painful death. We both need to breathe again. I don't want divorce but I see no other option. There has been no resolution. If we don't part ways, we will just remain in this painful, hellish place, as we always do.

I grab a paper and pen and start to scrawl:

Two roads diverge
Which will I choose?
Both roads feel like I will lose.
Each one a release, each one a prison
This is not a light decision.
My heart will break down either road
Which break to choose I hardly know.
But choose I must, and cry I will
Pain is the price for daring to heal.

I put down my pen and roll over.
Exhausted, sleep engulfs me.

Dream of Death

I am laying on the floor in some kind of a healing center. Two strange women are standing over me. One touches my throat and says, "You'll be dead in six months."

I wake in a panic.

One more dream about death. I've had many over the last several months. These dreams scare me because I've been sick with repeated throat infections for the last six months, really sick. I don't know why I can't seem to get better. When the throat infections go away, horrible fatigue sets in. I have no energy and can't seem to accomplish anything. I've also been having terrible lower back and sciatic nerve pain that makes it hard to do anything. As if it weren't already bad enough, these maladies are really affecting my marriage. Matt has lost patience for my repeated illnesses and we have constant contentious arguments.

Why did I come home?

I finally go to the doctor for testing. I'm sure I have mononucleosis or Chronic Fatigue Syndrome, but the tests show nothing. I am diagnosed with a simple throat infection. Still, I can't help but wonder if my dream was prophetic. I have been under so much stress for so long, how can I not have a disease or chronic illness? Am I dying?

I bought a book a few months ago called *Escape 101*. I was feeling completely desperate to . . . escape! I still feel it. I want to move to a new house or go on sabbatical or something! I have been painting the walls, purging the house of junk and getting the house ready to sell, even though I was sick. That is how badly I want change. I need expansion and meaning in my life. I need my own money so I can feel some independence in my marriage. I need to feel like I am not controlled by my circumstances. I know I am just looking for something to quell the anxiety of yet another self-betrayal. We should have gone through with the divorce. I should never have come home and returned to a dying and draining relationship. I feel so confused and helpless.

Another Decision

"I want to do a pageant," says my 14-year old, Chelsey. "I've been looking Online but can't find anything for girls younger than 16. Will you help me?"

This isn't the first time I've heard those words. Ever since I did the Mrs. Utah pageant last year, she has been periodically mentioning this. I'm not really excited about her doing a pageant. Pageants can be great and healing, or they can wreak havoc on your self-esteem. I'm not sure it will be a totally positive thing for her at the teen level. Still, I sit down at the computer and run a Goggle search with her. The results come up.

"I've never seen this one and I've run this search a bunch of times," she says.

We follow a few links and I begin to read aloud, "The US Continental pageant will be held in November—"

"And the age limit?" She cuts me off with an anticipation-filled voice.

"Thirteen."

"That means I can do it!" Her face is beaming.

I slink down in my chair. "*Great*," I say, as I try to hide my sarcasm.

"Hey, look," she grabs the mouse from me and scrolls to another part of the screen. "They have a Mrs. and a Ms. division.

We investigate the website for awhile and discover that all three divisions compete on the same stage on the same night.

"Will you do it with me?" The glow on my daughter's face tugs at my heart. "You already have most of the things we'll need." Her eyebrows are raised in excitement. "Besides, you said you might do another pageant someday."

It is obvious to me that this is something she really wants, maybe even needs, to experience. Who am I to tell her no? But what about me? Do I really want to try again?

I am at a place where I am at peace with my past pageant experience. I have been content for some time now, like I never need to compete again. But something stirs within me. Maybe I could do it . . . just one more time.

"Okay," I relent.

"Yeeees!" Her squeals fill the kitchen and bounce off the walls as she leaps out of her chair, grabbing her cell phone to call her friends with the news.

November it is. This could be a great mother-daughter experience. So why am I feeling anxious?

Separation by Degrees

I skip down the stairs to grab a bag of frozen vegetables from the freezer in the garage. Kale, Chelsey and Matt are watching a movie in the family room and laughing. I pause to watch for a minute with them.

"You've gotta see this one part, Mom," Kale says. "Can we rewind it for her?"

"Sure," says Matt.

They rewind the scene and we watch. It is funny.

I sit down to enjoy the show, but then suddenly bolt to my feet and race up the stairs remembering I had left a pan of oil on the hot burner!

The kitchen is foggy. A few more minutes and we probably would've had a fire! With a sigh of relief, I grab the pan and, using all the genius of a gnat, put it under a running faucet. The smoke detectors scream as the room fills with thick smoke.

I open the patio door and kitchen windows, turning on the fans as Matt races upstairs, "What's going on up here?"

An argument ensues that is too ugly and too ridiculous to relate, but the pattern of criticism and intolerance for mistakes is played out as usual, with more verbal vehemence than usual.

I finish making dinner, feed my family and quietly pack my bags . . . again.

I'm at mom's house sobbing on the familiar guest room bed. I can't go back this time. I really do love Matt but we just can't keep doing this.

I will be the first to admit that I haven't always been the best wife. In my own way, I have punished him for hurting me by blaming him for my unhappiness and lack of success. But really, I have chosen to be who I have become, and I can only blame myself for that.

On the flip side, his resentment about his decision to marry me started very early in our relationship and I didn't understand it. I still don't. I was so young that I didn't know how to react or how to protect myself emotionally from his withdrawal and I was profoundly hurt by it. Despite this, I look back now and know that I have loved him our whole marriage. I wouldn't have sacrificed so much if I didn't, but love is such an intimate and sacred gift that when it's rejected, it is so very painful and personal. That is why the scars of love are the scars that run deepest in the human heart.

I set down my pen and calm myself by taking even breaths. I think of a lifetime of contention and fighting every day in defense of a spirit that frequently feels violated and I am hopeless and discouraged.

Picking up my pen again, I write Matt a letter. It becomes a letter of apology, regret, gratitude and love—a goodbye. Divorce is the hardest thing I have ever had to do. I take marriage very seriously. It is a covenant between me, my spouse and God. It requires sacrifice, humility and love. In an attempt to save our marriage, I have sacrificed my own happiness over the years, but it hasn't been enough. I couldn't save us no matter how hard I tried. I have not been perfect, but I have given everything I could to the point of unhealthy giving. And I have fought tooth and nail to reclaim the dignity and self-respect I lost trying to save and win the heart of a man who never wanted to be won or saved. I think the only way he can be saved is if I leave.

Mirrors

Matt and I are talking tonight about our biggest issues. Every time I bring up divorce or leave, he somehow convinces me to come home and not pursue it, but we both know nothing is ever going to change. I find it odd that he has been asking for a divorce for so many years but now that I am asking, he doesn't seem to want it.

Confusing.

Still, I am home again.

The conversation continues easily for awhile, until I bring up the issue of my looks.

"This isn't a free for all where you can ask anything you want," he says with a sudden attitude.

"I think you owe it to me to be honest with me," I say.

I already know what's coming, but I'm hoping for a shift, a miracle, some reason to justify giving it one more try.

"I just don't like your nose. I can tolerate it, but . . . "

"Tolerate it?" My stomach churns. I don't want to be *tolerated* by my spouse. I want to feel, *to know* that I am beautiful to him. Is that so wrong? In my mind, you should never marry someone who has a physical feature so bothersome that you have to tolerate it.

I can live with the fact that we don't believe the same things anymore. I have proved that I can live through personal hell and still be a devoted and loving spouse in many ways, but I cannot live with being *tolerated* by the man who is supposed to love me and accept me unconditionally. I know I am not a perfect wife, but I have never withheld love based on physical appearance, or any other condition. Why can't he just accept me how I am? Have we really stayed this stuck all these years?

I go to bed deeply hurt.

The next morning, I am doing a Jillian Michaels workout, during which she says, "You have to push through the pain, that's when change happens."

"I want to change, God," I cry out loud. "I want to push through this pain. I am tired of hurting." I drop to my knees. "It seems like the more I heal, the more I hurt. Why, God? Why?"

Experience has taught me that desperate pleas to Heaven often bring clarity and answers in direct proportion to the desperation of the plea. The more open to hearing answers (even the ugly ones), the more likely an answer will come.

"God, every time I start to recover myself and gain confidence I get injured emotionally by Matt and I end up at square one."

I listen to the silence. Words come to my mind, "Every time you start to recover yourself and gain confidence you engage Matt, and push his buttons to reveal hurtful things about you so that you can justify blame and avoid the pain of healing."

I catch my breath. "Oh! He is mirror," I whisper out loud.

My mind is flooded with understanding. Last night's hurtful conversation was my fault. I was the one who insisted that he answer my question when I already knew what his answer would be. The pain of his honest reply merely reflected back to me my own painful truth, that I am the one who can't accept me. I am the one who won't see my beauty. Matt simply validated my own worst fears and beliefs.

I'm not sure what to do with this information, but I know I have to keep healing. I have to heal the pain I've attached to Matt and accept accountability for it. But how do I change it? And if I do, will it change anything between us?

Backing Out

Things have been crazy the last several months. The kids and I have moved out three times this year, and moved back three times. Everyone is sick of the uncertainty. The kids are even telling us to just "get a divorce already." I'm overwhelmed.

"I'm dropping out of the pageant," I tell my daughter. My heart is heavy as I see her face fill with disappointment. "You can still do it though," I reassure her.

"Why?" She is suddenly angry. "Why are you dropping out? I thought you wanted to do this with me."

"I do, but I can't really compete in a Mrs. Pageant when I don't even know what's going to happen with my marriage."

She shrugs her shoulders in resignation, appearing to understand my reasoning.

I know I have ruined her vision of this experience, but I don't know what else to do.

I sit down at the computer and send an email to the director of the pageant telling her I can no longer compete because of life challenges. I push send and try to wipe the concern from my mind. I can't help feeling bad for not competing. There has been one unanswered question on my mind ever since I decided to try for a crown again.

What if???

Freedom Behind Bars

The last two days have been emotional hell. I just can't seem to break free of this vacillating prison of indecision regarding divorce. Neither choice before me is acceptable. Both choices are excruciating. I feel broken, weak and vulnerable. I feel desperate to hear God's direction and yet terrified of his words. Fortunately and unfortunately, I get no answer from Him.

I struggle through the weeks, feeling weary. I can feel my body trying to get sick again. Several friends and neighbors suddenly appear more prominently in my life, stepping into support roles at this most difficult crossroads and I feel truly grateful for their love.

"You need to let go of Matt," my dear friend, Anna, says to me one afternoon as we talk. "You must stop trying to save him. Let him face the consequences of his decisions because they are his to bear. You are only enabling him."

I sigh with resignation and frustration. I know she is right, but what about me and my issues? Is he enabling me too? Can I justify leaving if my issues remain unhealed? Is that even fair? Do my issues even have a chance of healing if I stay?

"I was never able to change my depression or other problems . . .," Anna explains, "until my husband stepped back, left me alone and stopped trying to save me."

"Yeah, but he didn't divorce you."

"If you really, truly love Matt, then you will let him learn by experience and stop interfering. That is true love and true sacrifice. How that looks, whether through divorce or not, is up to you." She shrugs.

In the months that follow, I crawl through deeper and darker struggles of decision, seeking desperately for understanding. I have created a prison for myself in this relationship with Matt, and I don't know how to change it or get out of it. Is it possible to experience release, even while in prison? Is there some way to break through all the pain and oppression I am feeling?

And if I succeed in doing so, will I be able to stay in my marriage and keep my family together?

I think of some of my heroes: Corrie Ten Boom, Vicktor Fankl, Nelson Mandela all of whom experienced physical prisons and deep deprivations and survived. Even while incarcerated, they all became stronger. I must know how this is done! Is freedom possible for someone in an emotional prison?

I begin reading about love, tolerance and justice and the proper balance of those things. I review my relationship and how I have applied these principles either properly or improperly with Matt. The line of what is right is fuzzy. I write daily in my journal and weigh what I am learning in every spare moment of free time I can find. This has become a consuming quest.

Divorce is not a trivial thing for me. I must know that I have done everything that I possibly can to save my marriage, and that I am making this choice from a clear place, unsullied by emotion, ignorance or selfishness on my part.

As time passes, I find my heart opening back up to Matt. My mind becomes clearer on what I need to create happiness for myself and I begin taking greater accountability for my behaviors and mistakes. Still, issues between Matt and I keep coming up from which I do not know how to detach. The negative patterns we have built in our relationship are too ingrained and create huge problems for us.

Things start to unravel again. From one day to the next, I'm on a yo-yo, up and down, depending on Matt's moods and tolerance level. I continue to search passionately for the elusive understanding that creates freedom behind bars. I know it's a perception, a power of the mind, but it escapes me no matter how hard I try to find it.

I visit my friend Anna, who is a spiritual-based energy healer, for guidance and understanding.

"As you engage in Matt's energy, you carry some of his problems for him. He counts on that. You have to quit engaging and let go," she states.

I know she is right.

The months pass, and then one day it happens. I am on my knees praying and suddenly the light goes on. I get it!

And the shift is profound.

It is everything I already understand with my head, but suddenly my heart and head have aligned. I am free! And I feel it physically, not just emotionally. It is not something I can fully explain, but I feel enlightened and expansive. I clearly see what stuff is mine in the marriage and what is his, with no emotion or ego, just understanding.

A sense of forgiveness swells within my heart like an overwhelming wave. Gratitude washes over me, cleansing me from the chains of a self-imposed prison. Though my situation hasn't changed, my entire world has. I am free to see the situation for what it is, without bars, neutral and detached. I don't need to justify my decision based on behaviors or emotions. I can make my decision from a place of clarity and peaceful resolve, knowing, feeling and understanding what is best for both of us.

I have found freedom amidst challenge and it feels amazing!

The Gift of Beauty and Release

It is my birthday today and it's been a relatively peaceful morning. I had some great breakthroughs about safety and fear while journaling this morning.

My dear friend Anna, who has helped me through so much, stops by with a little gift and Happy Birthday wishes. Small talk turns to deep talk and I start crying. She immediately steps into a healer role.

"Do you have any fat crayons?" She asks.

I wrinkle my brow, puzzled by her question.

"No. I have some regular crayons though."

"Okay, those will do, but next time you're at the store buy some fat crayons, they hold up better for this."

I rise from the couch to get the crayons, wondering what she could possibly need them for.

"And grab a notebook or paper, too," she adds as I ascend the stairs.

A few minutes later, I return with the supplies.

At her direction, I choose a color, puke green. I start scribbling hard on the page.

"Harder," she instructs. "Scribble harder."

I do so, feeling a little foolish; then the crayon snaps.

"That's good," she says. "Keep going."

We do this for several minutes and with several colors, then look at my creations. They are ugly.

"All this was inside of you," she says, pointing to the page.

I shudder at the black color covering the page.

"Now that the emotion is outside of you the words can come out. What do you feel?"

I think for a moment, "Fear."

"What are you afraid of?" She asks.

"Failure."

"Failure of what?"

My eyes begin to sting with tears. "I fear the failure of the most important and sacred of commitments I've ever made," I swallow hard. "Divorce is proof of that failure."

We are both quiet while I digest the depth of my fears and what they mean to me.

"What else?" She asks slowly.

"I feel unworthy."

"Of what?"

"Unconditional love." I try and hold back the dam of tears I feel behind my eyes. "So many people have stepped up over these last few months and served me and my family in ways I can never repay. I don't deserve such kindness. "

"Why not?" She looks truly concerned.

I am silent, swallowing hard to prevent the sobs pressing for escape.

She waits for my response.

"I believe . . . ," my voice breaks. "I believe I have to be perfect to deserve such kindness."

"Ahhh," she says. "Do you know that you are worthy and beautiful?"

I shake my head back and forth in disagreement.

"I want you to do something," she says as she stands. "I want you to visualize yourself cutting away the lies that you are hiding behind and step forward into the truth." She takes my hand, raising me to my feet and then guides me forward through symbolic steps as she speaks.

I instantly recoil from the exercise as Matt steps through the front door.

Anna acts as if nothing has changed, as if we are still alone. She says, "I want you to repeat after me. *I am glorious and beautiful.*"

I cannot say it. It would have been hard enough saying it without Matt in the adjacent kitchen, but knowing he is there and can hear us, and knowing that he doesn't believe those things about me, leaves me speechless.

"Repeat after me," Anna coaxes again.

I shake my head in protest. How can I say such things within earshot of the man who did so much to nourish my negative beliefs?

"I can't do it," I whisper. I feel like my voice box is surrounded by an invisible cage.

"You've got to do this," Anna says insistently with tears in her eyes.

"I can't," I whisper again, tears streaming down my face.

"You've got to, or you'll never be free," she insists.

I stand frozen for what seems like an eternity.

"I am glorious and beautiful," I whisper, without a drop of conviction in my voice.

She nods, "Louder."

I repeat the words, still no conviction.

"Again," she directs.

I muster some conviction and try again; we both know I am holding back.

"Jennifer, when you truly believe this, when you truly love yourself, people will see it. You will be free to truly love them, and this will give them permission to love themselves."

I cry.

We hug.

She leaves and I know in my heart that I am the only obstacle standing in my way of happiness, not Matt, not my circumstances, just me.

A few days later, I am once again talking with Anna at church. She mentions my inability to repeat the affirmation of beauty and worth. "What was that about?" She asks.

"I couldn't say it with *him* in the room."

"I know," is her reply. "I just wanted to make sure you knew. In all relationships, even unhealthy ones, an invisible cord is created between two people. This cord gets thicker with each positive or negative interaction. You have got to cut that cord and let your husband go."

I start to cry.

"I know you've received your answer," she says. "So why are you fighting it?"

I begin to sob. She is right. I have known I should leave for a long time but I just haven't been able to accept that fact because I am terrified. I don't trust my own judgment. What if I make the wrong decision? What if I can't take care of myself? What if I am too weak?

"You and Matt are keeping each other locked in unhealthy and negative patterns. If you've received your answer, then you need to go so you can both heal." She squeezes my hand and leaves the room.

I sit alone in a pew in the empty chapel for awhile, letting the reality of this conscious acknowledgment surge through my bones, no fighting or resistance, just feeling my feelings.

The next morning, I stand in the shower as heaving sobs escape my lungs. I visualize Matt, seeing the cord that is connecting us. As the visualization continues, I take a huge pair of scissors—tell Matt I love him—and through more sobs and a face drenched in salt tears and water, I picture myself cutting this binding cord. I take the loose end, the one attached to Matt, and hand it to God, where it belongs.

Grieving sobs are finally followed by release.

It is finished.

Transformation in White

A few months after I decided to compete in a pageant with my daughter (and before I dropped out), I scoured the internet looking for the perfect evening gown. I knew I wanted gold fabric with ornate beading and rhinestones. I found several dress designs I liked but everything was too expensive so I decided to make my gown.

My daughter and I went to a fabric shop one day. I was prepared to buy the beautiful gold fabric I found, but they didn't have enough. I waited in an eternal line for some assistance because they told me I could order the fabric and they would call me when it came in. The line took so long that I decided against ordering it and we left the store.

In the weeks that followed, every time I thought about my gown I got this distinct feeling that I should wait to pursue a purchase, so I listened to my intuition and waited.

As I was cleaning out the basement one day, purging the physical junk from my life, I came across my wedding gown. It had been hanging in a bag for 18 years. I pulled it out and found it still as white as the day I wore it!

I cringed. "I can't believe I ever wore this thing," I said aloud.

I didn't think it was ugly when I wore it, but looking back I can't fathom why I ever chose it. It was a typical 1990s princess gown with a heavily beaded bodice, sweetheart neckline, huge puffy sleeves that tapered to a point at the wrist, and an enormous full skirt with an equally enormous bow on the back.

I debated what to do with the gown. I could donate it to somebody's Halloween clothing stash. Or I could give it to the local thrift store. I certainly didn't want to keep it. I am sentimental, but not that sentimental. All it was doing was taking up space and my daughter certainly was never going to wear it.

"That thing?" She scoffed, when I asked her if she wanted it. "No offense, Mom, but . . . ugh, no thanks." She shivered.

I had to laugh.

A sudden stroke of genius (or madness??) seized me as I held the gown, debating its fate. What if I turned this dress into my pageant gown? It would only require the cost of a few rhinestones and beads! The idea thrilled me. As a seamstress of 20 plus years, I had always wanted to make a custom beaded gown!

I grabbed a pattern from my stash, gathered my sewing supplies and began to work.

Some might call it sacrilege to cut up your own wedding gown. Others might call it the vengeful act of an unhappy wife. But this was neither for me. It was simply an economic maneuver that would provide me a lovely gown at a fraction of the cost of a purchased one and add a check-mark on my Bucket List. So I cut up the gown and put it in a drawer with the intention of finishing it over the next several months, but it didn't happen.

After Matt and I separated the last time, and I returned home, I dropped out of the pageant. I needed to focus on healing more than on competing. Still, I felt a compulsion to finish the gown, even though I'd have no practical use for it.

So I finally did finish it.

A few days ago, I was sitting in my room folding clothes when a random thought about the pageant sneaked into my head. "What if I'm missing an opportunity here?" I then chastised myself for even thinking such a thought. Surely I can't re-enter the pageant after I had dropped out! I am divorcing!

That very afternoon, I receive an email in my box from the director of the pageant. "Hey Jen, I was wondering if you are considering competing. We've moved the pageant to March because of some venue complications. I think you'd do awesome. Let me know."

I stared at the email in shock. I don't believe in coincidences. There had to be a reason for the timing of this message.

I wrote her back and explained my situation.

Today, she responded by telling me that there is a Ms. Division for women of any marital status and that I can change my entry to that division. I then sent her an email recommitting to competing in the new category. I already had a gown. Why not?

Tonight, I sit in the big green recliner in my office/craft room with my finished gown gracefully draping the dress-form in the corner of the room. I am talking on the phone with my mom, explaining to her the process of the gown's creation and my sense of accomplishment.

It has been an incredible labor of love. I had to cut out the new gown from the skirt of the old gown with extreme precision in order to have enough fabric to even create it. Due to months of stress surrounding the divorce process, I've lost a lot of weight and have had to make considerable alterations in the size and shape of the gown, resulting in *a lot* of unpicking and re-sewing. Surprisingly, I never became impatient through the process. Having several decades of sewing experience, I am very familiar with the positive results of patience, and somehow this project drew forth a natural, deep and abiding patience in me whenever I worked on it. It was almost therapeutic.

"That's interesting that your pageant gown was once your wedding dress and now it's completely transformed," my mom says. "That's very symbolic."

She's right! I have transformed that dress—that large, ornate, cumbersome dress—through painstaking re-construction, seemingly never-ending alterations and problems. I have done so, with patience, over time. I persevered and now the gown is a whole new creation, just like me.

My new gown is simpler and more elegant, with just the right amount of sparkle. With a crown and wings (both treasured symbols) embellishing it, the gown is complete. It has become a representation of the refining process I have been through. And although I have further yet to go, I have worked hard for the last five years to face and heal my issues. As a result, I have discovered myself. I have found the strength to make necessary changes in my life. I have honored my inner knowing and my boundaries, and I have learned to make decisions. In short, I have learned to love myself. Though I still struggle to fully embrace my beauty, I can feel that truth working on me internally.

Good things are ahead.

I can feel it!

Tiny Crown

I moved into my parent's house with the kids yesterday. It was an abrupt move, but necessary. It has been a huge blessing to leave sooner than anticipated. There is much to be worked out and I still have no answers about my life ahead. This has been a complete act of faith, a complete step into the darkness, but I feel good.

After a few weeks of decompression, Chelsey and I hit pageant preparation hard. We have 30 days until the competition. I still have wardrobe pieces to sew, my website to revamp, my walk to practice and interview questions to rehearse. I also need headshots and to complete my written biography for the judges to review. There is so much to do!

Several weeks pass.

Tonight, I am at a pageant rehearsal with Chelsey where we are practicing walking patterns for the stage. The current title holders decide to hold a little competition among the contestants. We are to walk the "stage" (someone's living room) as if we are competing. I feel a little self-conscious, but decide that it's now or never—either suck up the confidence or miss another opportunity, maybe my last one. So I walk my walk, look the "judges" in the eye and smile my best pageant smile.

Each woman and teen takes her turn and then waits for the results.

A few minutes later, I stand with two other semi-finalists. I hadn't expected to be one of them! My confidence increases. We are asked to walk the stage again so a winner can be chosen.

Five minutes later, my name is called and I am handed a tiny collectors crown as the prize.

After a long night's rehearsal, I climb into bed, gazing at the tiny crown that now sits on the dresser in my bedroom. It's a reminder that I do have what it takes to compete in, and even win, this pageant. I keep this mini-crown in sight as a symbol of my potential and good things to come.

Be Who You Are

"Ahh-choo!"

My eyes water from the seismic force of a sneeze. My cosmetologist sister is wrapping my head in foils, highlighting my hair for the pageant. I am seriously sick with the seasonal flu and have filled an entire grocery sack with gooey Kleenexes from my drippy eyes and nose. My entire body is aching. I feel terrible. Why did I have to get sick the day before the pageant?!

A few hours later, my hair has turned out great, but the hair extensions I bought won't work and they can't be exchanged. I can't afford to buy new ones either. I will have to make do with my own limp, fine hair. Not the best look for stage, but I can't do anything about it now.

When my alarm goes off the next morning, I feel like a Mac truck has run over me. It is interview day. My illness is slightly improved but I can't seem to rub the sleep from my right eye. It feels fat and swollen.

"Are you kidding me?!" I exclaim as I look in the mirror with horror and see the infection.

"What's wrong?" My mom yells from the kitchen.

"I have pink eye!"

My mom digs through her medicine box and finds an old prescription that I start using immediately, but in the afternoon, my heart is palpitating and my nerves are frazzled with frustration and stress. Not only can I not wear my false eyelashes to the judge's interviews because of the infection, I can't even get my eye makeup to stick to my skin! We are supposed to present our best selves! Why won't anything work for me?!

After three complete face washes and three attempts at makeup application, I throw my eyeliner on the counter and my hands in the air. "I give up!"

I have never looked good or felt confident without makeup and now here I am going to compete in a *beauty* pageant looking like I'd put no effort into my appearance. I sigh with frustration and finally surrender to the fact that I can't change this circumstance.

In my bedroom I kneel next to my bed and pray. "God, please help me to get through this and feel good about myself."

A thought, like a quiet, peaceful whisper comes into my mind, "Just be who you are, Jen. Just be who you are."

I return to the bathroom mirror, look at my minimal makeup and take one last look at my wardrobe. I have chosen a white blouse with tiny black polka dots and a slim shiny black belt that accentuates my waist. This is paired with a black pencil skirt and black heels. My overall statement is understated for sure, but really, that's who I am. I embrace it, yell to Chelsey that we need to leave, and head for the car.

We sit in the hotel foyer with the other contestants for hours, waiting for our turn to meet with the judges. I finally get to meet the other Ms. contestants who were absent from the workshops and luncheon. They are very nice and very beautiful. Their wardrobe choices are stunning and they definitely look like pageant winners. One looks like a Barbie doll and another like Carrie Underwood's twin!

As we line up outside the door for our turn in the judge's room, I am placed in between these two gorgeous women. I chuckle to myself at how odd I must appear standing between them. It reminds me of the old Sesame Street song,

One of these things is not like the other
One of these things just doesn't belong

Interestingly, I am uncharacteristically calm in their presence. A few years ago, I would have been comparing myself to them in every way until I had pulverized my self-confidence to dust, but not tonight. Whether it's the lack of energy from illness or something else, I feel no need to be anything other than what I am, and that feels really good.

Interviews are five-minute one-on-ones with each judge. We rotate from table to table when "time" is called. My interviews are very positive and I leave the room feeling really great.

"I absolutely love the judges you chose," I say to the judge's chairperson in the lobby. "They are such wonderful people!"

She smiles and hugs me in response, thanking me for the compliment.

I feel love within me and emanating from me. I am so calm in a situation that should inspire fear within me, and has in the past. It really doesn't matter what happens when all this is over because I have found a far greater prize than the crown.

I have found love.

I head straight to bed when we get home and lay with my thoughts for awhile. Although I feel detached from the outcome of the pageant, I continue to hold onto the desire to win. I can feel that desire in my heart and it is strong. I want to share my platform and the things I have learned with other women and girls who might be struggling with similar issues. I know that I have done all I can to prepare, my very best under the circumstances, and I must let go of the outcome.

Release is always a paradoxical phenomenon. Suspending one's desires to a point of detachment and yet still maintaining motivation to do your best is a balancing act. But there is a peaceful place between the two and I return to it tonight to maintain a sense of peaceful empowerment for the remainder of the competition.

"I release the outcome to you, God," I whisper into the night. "But it would be amazingly awesome if Chelsey and I could win together. If not, Thy will be done."

I feel the desire.

I feel the release.

I fall asleep.

Daring to Live and Love

As if being sick wasn't enough, I have started my period. What more could a girl ask for on pageant day!? And I'm wearing a white gown! Of course!! On top of that, my spray tan hasn't exactly turned out the way I expected and has essentially worn off. So now I will be sheet white on stage with limp hair, the flu and menstruating. Can it get any worse?!

Annoyed, I pack my things, making sure Chelsey and I have everything we need for the long day ahead.

I pray and take my bloated, cramping body to rehearsal.

On the way, we stop off at the hotel where the current title holders are staying and get a touch-up tan, which doesn't exactly work out either. Because the tan needs to dry, I can't wear a bra or anything tight, so I throw on a huge t-shirt and ugly sweats.

At rehearsal we begin practicing walking patterns. Wouldn't you know that because I am now wearing heels with my ugly sweats and a t-shirt the photographer decides to start shooting scenes from our practice! I am braless, bloated, cramping, with no makeup and my hair pulled back. I finally ask her not to direct the camera at me because this is not how I want to be captured for posterity.

Thankfully, she obliges.

As we proceed with practice, my body decides to violently start coughing up phlegm. I have to leave the room because I am hacking so forcefully, without reprieve, that I am both embarrassed and disruptive. Never in my life have I coughed so long or so hard.

The hours pass and suddenly it's transformation time. Fortunate to live so close to the pageant venue, Chelsey and I head home to get ready. My eye has calmed down a bit from yesterday, so at least my makeup and eyelashes stick this time! The evening passes relatively quickly. I am still waiting for nerves that never come.

We head to the venue and before I know it, we are onstage performing opening number, which passes like a blur. Then it's swimwear for the teens and fitness wear for the Ms. and Mrs. Contestants. I step onto the stage feeling totally alive. Miraculously, my energy has returned and I am lit up from the inside, like I was never sick.

The backstage side of a pageant is always fast. We rush around changing wardrobe, fixing hair and makeup, waiting for our cues to take the stage. When mine comes for the Evening Gown part of the competition, I step out under the stage lights and walk with ease. I take my time, pausing and smiling at both the judges and the audience. This is my moment. No one knows what it has taken to get here, to stand on this stage with the confidence and calm I am now feeling. No one knows how deep my fear of judgment has been, and how profoundly my beliefs about beauty have pained me in the past, how ugly or how wretched I have felt. And yet, none of these thoughts cross my conscious mind. In fact, my mind is blank. I only feel love and light emanating from me. I can't explain it. It just is.

For me, the theme of the night is peace, serenity and love. Each time I'm on stage, I feel connected to the audience and the judges through the invisible energy of love. It's amazing. Even the on-stage question, pulled randomly from a jar to answer spontaneously, is a serene experience, no nerves or anxiety, just calm.

By the end of the night, I know that I have done my very best. There is nothing about my performance I would change. I have been authentic in every respect and have achieved a victory that far outweighs any crown. I have stepped into love, felt it, exuded it and embraced it. My victory is within. I know who I am and I love myself, even with all my imperfections.

There is nervous chatter in the wings as the contestants wait anxiously to take their places on the stage for the winners to be announced. I look at Chelsey standing a few feet in front of me chatting with one of her new contestant friends. She has done a fabulous job tonight. She has been confident, showing personality and maturity beyond her years. I am so proud of her.

I offer one more silent prayer. "God, I feel good about tonight. I don't know what's going to happen out there, and I'm okay with whatever the outcome ends up being, but should I win, I really don't want the crown unless Chelsey wins it, too."

We step onto the stage and take our places to hear the results. Special prizes are announced in each division, with fitness and photogenic given out first.

"And Ms. Congeniality goes to . . . Jennifer Griffiths," the emcee says.

I take my place next to the former Ms. Utah, receive my award and smile for the camera. It is an honor to be chosen for the Congeniality Award. It means the other contestants felt you genuinely loved and cared about them through the event, which I did.

A few minutes later the teen division is announced. The second runner up is called and it isn't Chelsey. The first runner up is called . . . and it isn't Chelsey.

There are five girls left.

I am staring at Chelsey. I can see by her profile that she is chewing her lip, a nervous habit she has.

"And our new Miss Teen Utah is . . ."

Chelsey's name is called! She has won!

My hand grasps at my heart and my chest is bursting with delight. She has been given the crown! Her first pageant, and even while going through her parents' divorce! My legs are springs pointing in her direction. Though I want to wrap my arms around her and tell her how proud I am of her, I stay put, composed, as directed during rehearsal.

A crown is placed on her head, a sash over her shoulder and she is handed a bouquet. She walks across the stage waving, smiling and crying. My daughter, a queen! And I can't even give her a hug!!

I watch her exit the stage as the second runner up for the Ms. Division is announced. "Barbie" receives her award. I hold hands with my Carrie Underwood look-a-like friend. I can feel her hand shaking nervously. I am amazed at how calm I feel. At this moment of truth, I feel absolute peace.

There is a pause, silence in the theater, as the audience and contestants wait for the announcement.

The first runner up is called. I have won Ms. Utah!

Chelsey rushes back on stage and hugs me. "I don't care if I'm not supposed to be out here yet," she says to me.

We cry together. A crown is bobby pinned on my head, a sash draped across my shoulders and a bouquet of flowers placed in my arms as *Firework* by Katie Perry blasts from the speakers. I walk across the stage, smiling and waving. I look at the judges and mouth the words *Thank You*. I direct the same thought to God.

It's unbelievable! Chelsey and I have just been crowned on the same night, on the same stage, during the same pageant!

Matt is in the audience to witness his daughter, and me, win a beauty pageant. On the stage after the event, we take our last picture together as a family.

Two days later, our divorce is finalized.

Weddings are recorded with photographs and so are pageants. On the night of the pageant, a record of the ending to a very long story was made. There we stood, Matt and me, in my made-over wedding gown, at the end of our marriage. We had come full circle.

In Eastern cultures, white (the color of my gown) is the color of mourning. In Western culture, it is the color of purity and new beginnings. It was a moment of death and rebirth, mourning and celebration, an ending and a beginning.

People come into our lives to teach us. Those to whom we are closest stand to be our greatest teachers and, cause us the most pain. Sometimes the lessons from interacting with others can break us, but brokenness can lead to triumph. And although we must sometimes say goodbye to those we love the most, love never dies—it transforms.

Mine has been an incredible journey of pain, suffering, heartache and despair. But it also has been a journey of victory, both private and public. It has been a journey towards love, a journey of epic proportions, a battle for my own soul, revealing my true nature and worth. I have faced and fought darkness without a guarantee of success, cut away the lies and released the burdens I didn't need to carry. I have felt undermined by intense and irrational fear and then miraculously watched fear die because I dared to look it in the eye.

Eighteen years ago, I married a man who completely changed my life. I find it ironic that love would emerge so powerfully within me as it was simultaneously fading between the two of us.

I am filled with gratitude for all of the things I learned while I was married. The circumstances I experienced in my marriage opened an opportunity for me to choose to draw closer to my God, and to the true meaning of love more than anything else in my life has. I will always be deeply grateful for that.

Life doesn't always turn out the way we plan. But whatever ultimately leads to love, of self and others, is worth any sacrifice, any price, and any pain. When you find that love, your victory will far outweigh any crown that could ever be placed on your head.

I dared to get married, and it was a great challenge. I dared to get divorced and that was an even greater challenge. But daring to love myself has been the greatest challenge of all. And I wouldn't change a second of it.

~~THE END~~

THE BEGINNING

About the Dares

The Dares are a collection of lessons, principles and exercises I have applied in my own life on my journey toward learning to love myself and create positive change in my life. They are a form of life strategy, not therapy (see disclaimer at beginning of book), although many of the exercises could be, and possibly are, used by therapists.

You can do the Dares in almost any order, but I strongly recommend doing the first ten Dares in the order they are written to give you a foundation for progress.

The Dares are meant to help you create more body-mind-spirit-emotion awareness. Awareness is the key to change. The exercises are meant to help you evaluate habitual actions that could be robbing you of personal power, peace, happiness, joy, success, etc.

If you find yourself struggling with any Dare, ask yourself why and honestly evaluate any blocks you might have in connection with the Dare. If necessary, consult a therapist to work through difficult concepts together.

I recommend that you seek out supporting truths on each topic from other sources and especially in connection with your spiritual, worship or religious practices. Listen to your intuition and let it guide you. Your journey to powerful, positive change will be unique and divinely designed. The Dares are just a starting point.

Recognize that time is essential to creating new habits and coping with unearthed pain. Take as much time as you need with each dare to fully absorb and apply each concept. Set your own pace.

If you don't agree with something I've written, that's your prerogative. Find a version of what I have shared that does work for you, or scrap the Dares that don't resonate with your beliefs. In other words, find your own path and use the Dares as a template.

God bless you on your journey. And remember that you are beautiful. You are worthy. You are love.

Dare 1: It's All About Desire

"They key ingredient for change is desire—burning desire. Unless there is a deep hunger, a burning desire for changes you want to bring about in your life, these changes will not happen."
~Herbert Harris

"Change is hard because people overestimate the value of what they have—and underestimate the value of what they may gain by giving that up."
~James Belasco and Ralph Stayer

I knelt next to the couch in the den praying, telling God that I hated myself and I could no longer go on feeling that way. It was one of those desperate prayers, one of those "please-I'll-do-anything" prayers. I've come to understand that those kinds of prayers are always answered, but rarely in the way you hope or expect. You see, I begged God for release from my prison of self-loathing and then decided to take matters into my own hands. I decided the resolution to my plight was plastic surgery. Yes, that was the ticket! It had to be. A change of face would cure it all. Then I wouldn't have to feel horrible every time someone looked at me.

So I found a doctor and had a consultation. I was on my way!

Or so I thought.

A couple of unexpected events occurred during the following weeks and the cash I had for the surgery suddenly disappeared into other obligations.

Now what?!

I was miserable, unhappy and left with only two options. I could either wallow away in pain and sorrow or I could change. At that point, change seemed the kinder, less painful path. So I made the decision to heal from the inside out with no plastic surgery, no counterfeit solutions. I decided to tackle the dark abyss of self-hatred right at the source—my heart.

Only, I had no idea how to do that. YET.

As human beings, we are programmed to avoid pain and seek pleasure. Even if we're experiencing massive amounts of emotional pain, we will usually find ways to cope because the pain of change seems even more excruciating than what we are currently experiencing. It looked like this to me:

I hate myself and that hurts. It makes it impossible for me to accomplish anything truly fulfilling or to have fulfilling relationships. I feel bad all the time and have no confidence. BUT, the possibility of changing that reality seems even more painful and is full of unknowns, therefore, I'll just sit tight, wallowing in misery until I can't stand it anymore! Then hopefully something will change for me!

And that's exactly what I did; at least until I got to that point of "I can't stand it anymore" and realized that if it was going to change, I had to change it myself. At that point, I didn't care that it would be painful. I would accept the consequences. After all, they couldn't be any worse than what I was already experiencing, right?

What I have learned since that time is that change really comes down to two basic principles: desire and faith. Faith is more than a belief. It is motion; it is action.

What change really comes down to is: "How bad do you want it?" *And* "Are you willing to walk into the dark to get it?" And when I say walk that means ACTION.

Kneeling by that couch, I wanted release more than anything I had ever wanted before. I was broken and therefore, ready and willing to face the unknown. Not everyone feels the way I felt. Not everyone is that low. Perhaps you just want more self-confidence and more success in your endeavors but can't seem to manifest them. If you've experienced repeated "failures" at making changes in your life, then you may want to ask yourself a few questions:

- Do I *really* want it?
- How bad do I want it?
- What price am I willing to pay to get it?
- What is the payoff I get for *not* doing it?
- Why do I repeatedly fail to get what I want?

There comes a moment in most people's lives when their soul asks them to make a choice, to reach higher. You may want to, but for some reason you stand still. Why? Does the call seem too big? Too impossible? Is the change required too painful?

Small steps lead to mighty miracles, mighty change. I know. I've experienced it. I know that if you engage with true desire and consistent action, you will uncover personal growth and see changes in your life.

The truth is, whatever you desire and decide to experience in life is what you will receive—if you dare to do the work. No one can give it to you. It is your decision alone. This book is simply a call to action. Will you rise to the occasion? Will you finally show the world your wings? Do you want to be better tomorrow than you are today? Do you want to feel self-love, self-confidence and self-worth? Do you dare to give yourself those gifts? Do you dare to exercise the faith that small actions applied habitually can deliver big and lasting results?

Yes?

Then let's begin.

I dare you.

Today's Dare

I dare you to allow the desire to love yourself breathe within you.
Then let that desire work on you until it becomes a reality.
In the meantime . . .

Take a few minutes to write down one to three personal goals that you have consistently failed to manifest in your life. For example, I have wanted to learn a second language for years, but have failed to do so. I have also wanted to be better about getting up early but have failed to consistently pull that off. Why? Ask yourself the following questions in connection with your list:

1. On a scale of 1 to 10, how strong were your desires in connection with these goals?

2. Were your actions parallel with your desires? In other words, effort and desire are usually congruent. If your desire is weak your actions will follow.

3. Can you see a pattern emerge in connection to your "failures" in the thing(s) you've listed? Try not to judge yourself, but simply allow yourself to observe what has been. As you come to see yourself and your actions without judgment you will gain self-knowledge, which is the epitome of personal power. The goal here is to determine if lack of desire has been an issue for you in the past. Could lack of desire be an issue for you now as you embark on the journey to love yourself? Keep in mind that the admission of such a possibility is okay. Your desire will start to grow as you experience positive results along the way.

Dare 2: The Importance of Awareness

"Know Thyself"
~ Socrates

"Knowing others is intelligence; knowing yourself is true wisdom. Mastering others is strength; mastering yourself is true power."
~Lao Tzu

To say the least, 2003 was a horrible year. After years of criticism, reprimands and chastisements on everything from my opinions to my physical appearance to my feelings and personality, I had learned not to rock the boat. I kept most of my opinions to myself and had pretty much lost the essence of who I was. I tried to be something I thought I was supposed to be to please someone else.

Bad idea.

Conformity to the expectations of others, including media and culture can cause us to lose ourselves. We have to rediscover who we are—and love ourselves—before we can effectively actualize innate potential. Even a person who doesn't have conformity issues (and I don't know many who don't at some level) may not be operating from a place of awareness, conscious choice or personal power. It's just the nature of the beast to operate on autopilot, from our senses and habits, but this is not the empowering way to live.

So what's the remedy? What's to be done?

Consistent, small doses of self-discovery. This is done by creating self-awareness on many different levels. The main purpose of *The Love Yourself Dare* is to help you create awareness, because awareness equals personal power. Some may call it consciousness, or self-observation. You can call it whatever you like, but I will address it throughout the remainder of this book as awareness.

Dare 2: The Importance of Awareness

Most of us walk through life rarely observing our emotions, habits or tendencies. How can you know why you act and react the way you do if you don't observe yourself? You become like a feather in the wind, blown about to act or react solely based on moods and habits, or the whims and habits of other people. And that stinks. Talk about feeling out of control! And who can feel confident when they feel like all their power is outside themselves?

Knowing yourself is an act of bravery, a show of courage. To look within and face the rugged terrain inside is one of the most daring challenges of all. Doing battle with the subconscious, learning its moves, defenses and attacks empowers you to live from a place of choice rather than reaction, and that breeds confidence.

Today's Dare

I dare you to commit to becoming a self-aware individual by embracing and applying each of the dares contained in this book.
I dare you to commit to becoming confident and empowered through personal observation.
In addition . . .

In anticipation of the coming Dares, I challenge you to purchase a small notebook that will fit in your pocket or purse as well as some kind of larger notebook or journal to write in. Make it a priority to acquire these two things so you have a place to record and complete your Dares. Recording is a powerful and essential part of the journey toward personal change.

Dare 3: Lighten Up

"Who is more foolish? The child afraid of the dark or the man afraid of the light?
~Maurice Freehill

"Live in rooms full of light."
~Cornelius Celsus

A plant takes energy from the sun and converts it into nutrients in a process called photosynthesis. What happens when you cover the leaves of the plant and block out the light? Yep. That's right. The plant is denied essential energy and nutrients, and eventually dies. Light is that critical to its development.

Light is just as important to people, only most of us don't realize it.

As you probably already know from your school days science classes, light vibrates at a much faster or higher frequency than darkness. A search into the subject of vibrational frequencies will reveal that everything from the foods we eat, to the emotions we feel, to the cells in our bodies, registers at a particular frequency. Almonds, for instance, vibrate at a much higher frequency than your favorite candy bar. Fresh vegetables resonate at a higher frequency than canned vegetables. Positive emotions resonate higher than negative ones.

Whatever we take into our bodies affects our vibrational frequency (energy level), either raising it or lowering it. Have you ever noticed how when you eat certain foods, listen to certain music, or are around certain people your moods, and even your physical well-being shifts? The frequencies of those things are acting upon you, influencing you and changing you, albeit very subtly most of the time.

Again, light is a high frequency, dark a low frequency. A very simple way to help people grasp how their actions, moods, diet, thoughts, and beliefs are affecting them is to have them observe those things in terms of light and dark. If something lifts you, makes you healthier, more energized, it has a "light" effect on you. When it brings you down in any way, it has a "dark" effect on you.

If you think of your body as a container, what are you pouring into it each day? Light or darkness? Most of us are a mixture of both. However, the more light we "fill" ourselves with, the brighter we become. You've met people who just seem to radiate or glow, right? Their countenances seem to shine. Those people "hold" a lot of light. They do things that raise their vibration, and as a result, experience higher levels of confidence, radiance and joy than people who do not. So, although low levels of light won't quickly send you to your demise like a plant, it may affect your ability to feel good, confident, energized and empowered. I have personally experienced the confidence, clarity and happiness that accompany high vibration living, and it's a beautiful feeling.

Today's Dare
I dare you to consider whether you are living a life of
light or darkness.
In addition . . .

I dare you to do one thing today that adds light to your life—something that raises your energy level and lifts you. It could be exercise, a walk out in nature, drinking more water, spending time with someone who makes you feel amazing, or even a simple effort to refrain from criticizing yourself or another person. Positive actions equal light. So go ahead, live lighter. I dare you.

Dare 4: Record It

"Writing about one's own life, it is only when one writes about the most intimate and seemingly idiosyncratic details that one touches others."
~Susan Griffin

"I write constantly, but only in my journals. I have three of them: one for travel, one for home, and one I write in before bed. But the last thing I want is other people reading it . . ."
~Cameron Diaz

I hope you got a notebook for *The Love Yourself Dare* journey because we are going to start using it!

Two common concerns (a.k.a. excuses) that often come up when I suggest the concept of journal-keeping are:

1. "Someone might read it."

Yes, someone might. So hide it, or lock it up if you're worried about that.

2. "I hate writing. I can't write."

Then type it if you prefer, and keep it in an invisible file on your computer. Just know that writing by hand accesses a different part of your brain and is important in grounding and processing feelings.

Problem solved!

I don't mean to be insensitive to any real worries you may have about recording your experiences with *The Love Yourself Dare* but the fact remains that there is something very powerful about taking thoughts and putting them in a tangible form on paper. We can see and hear ourselves clearer than if those thoughts just remain floating around in our brains, unanchored to the page. When our thoughts are written, we can recognize patterns easier and remember things we might otherwise forget. Time has a distorting effect. If something is written down, you're more likely to remember it clearly and correctly. Also, seeing where you've been and where you currently are is huge! Sometimes we can't see our progress because it happens so subtly and over time. Recording proves progress. I read back over some of my journal entries and think "Wow, was I ever really that low? That insecure?" Yikes! There is no doubt about the leaps and bounds I've made in progress over time! It's in writing!

If you're not already sold on the idea, to help ease you into the idea of journaling, we are going to start simply. I'm not going to ask you to pour out your soul on the page—yet. I'd like you to just get used to recording for now, but what we record, even though it may seem simple, will be invaluable.

Today's Dare

I dare you to open up to the possibility that journaling could be a powerful tool on your journey toward self-love and confidence.

In addition . . .

Starting today, observe and record in your small, portable notebook the following:

1. How much water you drink each day.
2. What time you get up and go to bed.
3. Whether you exercised or not.
4. Also, record one overall word that describes the essence of your day (i.e. depressing, joyful, tiring, or stressful or whatever emotion first comes to mind.)

We will expand on this information later and look at what you've recorded in another dare. So be diligent. I dare you.

Dare 5: What's Water Got to Do With It?

"If there is magic on this planet, it is contained in water."
~Loran Eisely

"When the well is dry, we know the worth of water."
~Benjamin Franklin

Even if you don't belong to a religious denomination, I'm sure you're familiar with the story of The Creation of the World as recorded in Genesis of the Bible. As I was studying this story one day, looking for deeper meaning, I paused on Day Two. On this day, God divided the waters above from the waters below. I pondered on this for awhile, which lead me to study water vapor.

Water vapor is water in gas form. Mist, fog, clouds and precipitation such as snow, rain, sleet and hail are all forms of water that could not form without water vapor. Without water vapor, there would be no water cycle, and thus no life. Water in all its forms is essential and critical to our planet and its inhabitants.

In addition to the physical, tangible water sources (oceans, rivers and streams) we find on the earth, we also must have this invisible water vapor "above the earth." So in essence, on the second day, God divided the physical and spiritual waters—the seen and the unseen. From this basic science lesson, I took another testament of the dual nature of all things.

I'm sure you're familiar with the Eastern philosophy of yin and yang as opposites. According to this philosophy, if there is a physical body, there is also a spiritual body. It is essential to address both the physical and spiritual aspects of the self in the process of developing self-love, confidence and personal power. How can you live from a higher place if your mindset is purely based in the physical? The very virtues of hope, faith, beauty and potential are spiritual by nature. They are the abstract elements of the self and must be approached on that plane. It is in the combination of the abstract (spiritual) and concrete (physical) that balance and true beauty of self are achieved.

Let's shift gears for a moment.

According to Wikipedia, the earth is 70.9% water. And, depending on size, the human body is approximately 70% water. Human water makeup is basically equivalent to the earth's water makeup. And yet, how many of us drink enough water each day? How can your body perform all of its functions properly if it is deprived of precious water? What if the earth only cycled water occasionally? What droughts and other catastrophes would occur? We don't have a human body water cycle that takes care of itself. We have to physically put liquid into our bodies each day. And if we don't put enough, there are physical consequences such as dehydration and decreased brain function. Drinking enough water benefits your body in many ways. It is vital for the following:

- Transporting nutrients and oxygen into cells.
- Improving brain function. After all, the brain is 90% water.
- Moisturizing the air in the lungs.
- Aiding in metabolism.
- Helping organs absorb nutrients better.
- Regulating body temperature.
- Detoxifying.
- Protecting joints.

Who doesn't want these benefits? Seriously. Improved brain function? Better metabolism? Detoxification? Sweet! Sign me up! And it's just a glass away.

Today's Dare

If you haven't already considered it, open up to the idea of duality—the spiritual and physical.

In addition . . .

Yesterday, I asked you to start recording in your notebook how much water you are drinking each day. Continue doing this and, if you're not getting enough, make an effort to increase your water intake by at least one glass over the next few days. And then increase from there. If you need advice on how much water is right for you, find a trusted and reliable resource Online or talk to your doctor.

Dare 6: Love Withholds Judgment

*"We judge ourselves by what we feel capable of doing.
While others judge us by what we have already done."*
~Henry Wadsworth Longfellow

*"The secret of attraction is to love yourself. Attractive people judge neither
themselves nor others. They are open to gestures of love. They think about love, and
express their love in every action.
They know that love is not mere sentiment, but the ultimate truth
at the heart of the universe."*
~Deepak Chopra

After three separate promptings that I should enter a beauty pageant, I finally made the decision to compete in one . . . and I put it in writing.

Jan 24, 2008

I decided today to set a goal to enter a pageant next year. I set this goal once before a few years ago, but never did a thing to try and achieve it. I think I wasn't in the right place emotionally to take it on, but the thought has resurfaced. I think it's something I need to do. I don't have high hopes of winning because I'm really not physically "beautiful of face," but I have such a deep desire to be a person of substance and grace and I think having the goal to compete will help me reach my other goals. It will give me a deadline and a curriculum to work from. I have held such a stagnant position for a long time and I think that season is at an end. I can't be and do what God requires of me in my current state. I really need to begin to emerge from hiding and touch those things God would have me touch.

As my journal entry shows, I was struggling with some preconceived ideas about what I needed to be in order to compete and yet I was still crazy enough to commit to the task!

Jan. 25, 2008

So, I've decided to do the Mrs. Utah pageant next year. I need to go through with it, but naturally such a commitment is causing me distress. I am a far cry from pageant material so I've got to learn to see myself as a completely different person, so I can become so. This really is a crazy goal! I don't really think I'm supposed to be a titleholder, but I do think I'm supposed to learn all the things that I need to learn to compete, and competing will give me a reason to pursue and complete those smaller goals which I have tried to accomplish in the past but have failed to because I saw no reason, or rather, had no motivating factor to move me to action. Hopefully I won't freak out and quit.

Notice how I embraced the belief that I needed to become a "completely different person."

Mar, 14, 2008

I am still having a battle in my head about the pageant. I keep thinking that I'm too awkward of face (not pretty enough) and not educated enough. These are two huge hang-ups for me.

Mar. 25, 2008

I'm noticing that I really have issues with fearing people's opinions of me. I am deeply hampered by feelings of inadequacy.

Numerous journal entries throughout the rest of 2008 detail similar sentiments. I was really struggling with fear of judgment through the entire process of pageant preparation. Not only did I fear the judgments of other people, I religiously practiced harsh self-judgment. I guess I thought that if I judged myself first then somehow the judgments of others would be less painful. But that was pretty much "stinkin' thinkin'." Ultimately, facing the reality of competing in a beauty pageant brought up deep anxieties within me. BUT they were anxieties that my subconscious mind recognized that I was ready, and needed, to face. A part of me knew that if I was to overcome such deep insecurities, a pageant would put me face to face with them, and what better way to rid myself of them than to face them head on?

I competed against 20 of the most beautiful and successful married women in my state. When pageant night came, the house was sold out. Over 700 people attended, plus five judges, all of whom would be judging every woman who walked out on that stage. Hair, makeup, wardrobe, body type and size—everything would be scrutinized. Yes, I walked out into the lion's den and guess what? I survived! No, I didn't win. In fact, I didn't even make the top ten, but I won something better: dignity, self-respect and the ability to finally break through the fear of judgment. Walking out on that stage in the face of the very thing I feared was a liberating experience, and from that point, my healing journey progressed at light speed.

Certainly, I don't advocate pageant participation for everyone suffering from fear of judgment issues. After a pageant, there is a loss and healing process for every woman who does not walk away with the crown. For some, the experience can be a devastating blow to their self-worth rather than a healing experience. But for me, it was just what I needed.

The ability to suspend judgments about the self is such a critical skill to develop in fostering self-love. It starts with creating an awareness of our thoughts and actions. Once I had determined and committed to compete in the pageant, judgment after judgment surfaced for me and I was forced to face them. Not everyone needs such drastic motivation, but I did.

For the past few days of *The Love Yourself Dare*, we have been working on developing self-observation skills, which, in turn, develop self-awareness habits. Noticing when and how often you judge yourself is an important awareness to uncover. I didn't realize how constant my self-judgment (self-condemnation, really) was until I knew I would be forced to face the judgments of others in a public way. When I uncovered how deep and pervasive they were, and when I finally released the habitual action to judge myself, I was then freed to move into a place of power. This proclivity to negative self-judgment was a huge power drain for me and once addressed, allowed me to tap into strength and energy that previously had been eaten up in negativity.

Today's Dare

I dare you to put a mark in your notebook each time you catch a negative judgment about yourself or another person entering your thoughts or speech.

In addition . . .

I dare you to stop yourself when thinking or expressing a negative judgment. Try re-framing your words and turning that negative statement into a positive statement instead. The exercise of self-control is power in action.

Dare 7: Love Allows

"Listen, listen, listen
To my heart's song.
I will never forget you,
I will never forsake you."
~Paramahansa Yogananda

Judgment and allowing go hand in hand, supporting each other in the outcome of developing self-love. Yesterday, we addressed the suspension of judgment. This is facilitated through the process of allowing.

First, recognize that you have a right to feel the way you feel. Those feelings are just feelings and need to be felt in order to be released. The more we block and ignore our feelings, the longer they may persist. It's okay to feel, and yes, that includes your negative feelings. They are part of the human experience.

Unfortunately, we are conditioned to judge or condemn negative feelings when we feel them. That's why so many of us repress them, ignore them or placate them in various ways. The trick is to recognize when you are feeling a negative emotion, label it, sit with it for a few minutes and ALLOW it to exist. Allowing doesn't mean committing to feel that way forever. It simply means acknowledging that you feel a certain way in the moment. Nothing more. Nothing less. And feeling that way is okay. In essence, you are validating yourself and the normal human experience of feeling.

There is an excellent book called *I know I'm in There Somewhere* by Helene G. Brenner, Ph.D. that explains how to "sit with your feelings." I shared my experience doing this exercise earlier in Book II, in the chapter entitled *Sitting with the Enemy*. I shared this with you because this experience for me was pivotal in understanding how to allow myself to feel without judgment and to experience the subsequent liberation of listening to myself. I allowed images, words and thoughts to rise up into my conscious mind while relaxing and then withheld judgment regarding them. In turn, I learned some profound lessons about myself. This new awareness gave me power to take action. Before having this knowledge, I didn't know what to do because I didn't know what my problem was. Listening to and allowing feelings are mighty tools for self-reclamation and personal empowerment.

Today's Dare
I dare you to commit to allowing yourself to feel. I dare you to allow yourself to be human.
In addition . . .

I dare you to take a few quiet minutes to relax by yourself. Close your eyes and do one of two things, or both if you're ready:
1. Make note of any uncomfortable physical sensations your body is feeling.
2. Allow any feelings or words associated with those bodily ailments to rise to the surface of your mind.

If you feel any anxiety associated with this exercise, take a deep breath and recognize that what you are experiencing is just emotion. Feelings only hold the meanings we give to them. Try to suspend meaning from emotion and just feel, without running thoughts or scripts through your mind. In other words, try not to determine what your feelings mean; try not to define them. It's okay to label them in this exercise. For example, "I'm feeling angry." But try to leave it at that, just feel. If this gets too deep or difficult, then just stick with recognizing and recording the physical sensations in your body and save step two for another time, perhaps with a therapist. Journal your experience.

Dare 8: Love Breathes

"He lives most life who breathes most air."
~Elizabeth Barrett Browning

"Whenever I feel blue, I start breathing again."
~L. Frank Baum

May 25, 2009

I close my eyes and take a deep, long breath. Is this what it feels like to truly breathe? I can't remember. I haven't really breathed in so long. Here on the patio, it comes so easily, naturally. I don't even have to try. With each exhale, stress, anxiety and tension seem to dissipate, making room for beauty, peace and relaxation. It is a wonderful and long-neglected sensation.

We went to the beach this morning. The sound of the ocean was soothing and acted as a buffer to the noise on the shore. I watched the hypnotic waves, like great lungs of the Earth, breathing in and out, never ceasing, always changing, sometimes strong, sometimes shallow, but always constant. It was a reassuring sound, reminding me that life begins and abides with breath.

I tend to hold my breath when I am feeling anxious. It took several observations made by friends to bring this to my attention. No wonder I always feel so much tension in my shoulders! My muscles don't get enough oxygen! Still, I've done little to correct this problem. I know I need to change this unhealthy habit, but I've been too busy to address it. I don't have time to breath! How ridiculous is that? Perhaps if I took the time to breathe, I wouldn't feel so much stress.

One thing I have observed on my visit here is a pattern of thriving and flourishing. The combination of rainfall, humidity and sunshine obviously nourishes the environment and allows this vivacious plant life to thrive in abundance, its true radiance revealed. Things can't help but grow here, me included. And growth begins with awareness.

If I am not nourishing myself with something as essential and basic as full breaths of oxygen, how can I ever expect to flourish in my life? If I want a vibrant life, then I must find out what nourishes me on every level and apply it to my daily pattern of living.

I suppose it comes back to breathing. As I breathe, I relax. As I relax, I allow. I want to thrive, like the plants of the island. I want my life to be full of color and variety, full of beauty and peace. I want to flourish, but until I start breathing, until I start allowing, until I start viewing my whole world rather than that which I just choose to see, I will not be able to thrive. I must remember, and recover my ability to breathe in life, to breathe in those elements that will help me flourish.

I wrote the above as I sat on my patio journaling during a trip to Maui. It was a trip of many breakthroughs with much reflection and contemplation. I had never really considered breathing before; it's such an automatic process. In fact, for most of us, unless we have breathing problems, we take breathing for granted, never even considering the beautiful miracle it is.

Breathing affects everything in the body, and unless we are exercising or singing properly, most of us don't get deep, full breaths of oxygen. And yet, quality breathing is essential to beauty, abundance and peace. It's definitely something to start considering.

Today's Dare

I dare you to remember that breathing is essential to your well-being, and the quality of your breathing directly affects you on every level.

In addition . . .

In your portable notebook, I dare you to jot down any tension you feel accumulating in your body today. Are you breathing? Or is your breath shallow? Do you hold your breath when you get anxious? Do you sigh a lot? Monitor your breathing habits for a few days. If you're not breathing fully, make it a priority. Your body, your mind and your spirit will thank you for it!

I dare you to breathe.

Dare 9: Body Mapping

"My body was talking to me."
~Jerry Azumah

"Emotion always has its roots in the unconscious and manifests itself in the body."
~Irene Claremont de Castillejo

In fall 2005, I read a book that introduced me to Body Maps. I had never heard of this before, but found it to be a very enlightening and educating exercise.

The process of converting negative emotions and beliefs into positive ones is merely a process of creating self-awareness. Once we have this powerful self-awareness, we can then live from a place of choice, rather than a place of habitual action. As we monitor and observe our thoughts, emotions and physical sensations regularly, we become empowered to make choices that simply didn't exist before because we didn't understand what was really going on.

When you live on autopilot, your opportunities to exercise choice are severely limited. A body map is one way to help you develop the self-awareness that is required to be an active and fully-awake participant in your own life. When we are fully awake, life can be everything we ever dreamed and more because we realize that we have a choice in all things!

So how do you create a body map?

Go online to Wikipedia and search "File:outline-body.png" to get a printable body outline, or just draw a gingerbread man shape on a piece of paper. When you have a few minutes, grab a package of crayons and a comfortable seat with a hard surface you can work on.

Begin anywhere on the body outline. Color each body section according to how it feels to you. For example, if you start with your feet, concentrate on how they feel physically. What color do they feel like? What is the first color that comes to mind when you think of how your feet feel right now? Grab that color and fill in the feet portion of the outline with that color. Continue on until your body map is filled.

To take this exercise a step further, go back to each specific colored area and consider it again. What is the first word that comes to mind in association with this body part and color? Write it down, even if it seems unrelated or random. If a random word comes up, consider it in relation to the function of that specific body area. For example, your feet move forward, they symbolize direction and ability to act. They are the foundation the body stands on. Are any of these things significant in relation to your word? Consider the possible connections, problems and associations you hold personally with this area of the body or this word.

Next, write an overall statement of your impression of this body map to the side of your finished creation. What have you learned about yourself? This is a representation of your body today.

Several years ago I did a body map. My results were as follows:

Feet	White	Feel achy
Legs	Pink	Feel infirm
Gut	Brown	Feels crowded, dysfunctional
Torso	Light Blue	Feels undefined
Back	Red	Feels tense
Shoulders	Red	Feel tense
Arms	Orange	Feel strong
Throat	Orange	Feels free
Head	Grey	Feels heavy
Hands	Green	Feel useful

On the page I wrote, "How do I feel about this picture? Unsatisfied, it's ugly."

Our bodies and emotions are always changing. If you do a map next week, it will likely be different. If you do this exercise repeatedly and keep coming up with specific areas of color or repetitive words, it may be a cue from your subconscious mind that there is something you need to address or heal, either symbolically or physically in that area.

This exercise is a great one to help you understand how your physical body and emotional body connect specifically within you. On my own journey, I have come to understand that there are certain parts of my physical body that react to specific emotional stresses. I can pinpoint where in my body I hold fear and stress. I usually feel the physical sensation before anything else and that helps me recognize what is going on inside of me emotionally. Once recognized, I can ask myself some questions, get to the heart of the matter, make an empowered choice and move forward from a place of confidence and peace.

Our bodies, spirits and emotions are inseparably connected. They influence and affect each other. When you can recognize what repeated physical sensations mean to you, you have yet another powerful tool in your self-knowledge toolbox, and that's pretty cool!

Today's Dare
I dare you to remember that body, spirit and emotions are inseparably connected and affect one another.
In addition . . .

I dare you to create a body map.

Dare 10: Beliefs and Perceptions

"Within you right now is the power to do things you never dreamed possible. This power becomes available to you just as soon as you can change your beliefs."
~Unknown

"Every issue, belief, attitude or assumption is precisely the issue that stands between you and your relationship to another human being; and between you and yourself."
~Unknown

- I am ugly.
- I am unworthy of love.
- I was created to suffer.
- I am unacceptable.

These are some of the major beliefs that I walked around with for years. They were created through perceptions based on my experiences, emotions and self-talk, but those beliefs and perceptions were distorted. The "lenses" through which I viewed the world were cloudy. I have since learned to believe otherwise. I am beautiful. I am worthy of love. I was created for joy. I am acceptable, just the way I am, flaws and all.

Waking up every morning with the beliefs in the bulleted list above was drudgery. My days were heavy and full of pain. Waking up to my new beliefs is light. I feel energized and passionate about life. I feel like I have wings, like I can do anything. I still get down sometimes, but not for long because I have gained a certain level of mastery over my emotions, rather than letting my emotions control me. This process of self-mastery begins with awareness of beliefs. We must understand the power of beliefs and perceptions.

Let's define these terms as I am using them to assure we are on the same page.

- A belief is anything I hold as truth. *I am ugly. I am fat. People hate me.* These are examples of negative beliefs. I also hold many positive beliefs.
- Perceptions are the "lenses" through which I view the world. They are the way I see and interpret what is occurring around and within me. They feel like truth, but are not necessarily true.
- Experiences are external events and circumstances that combine with my perceptions and emotions to create my beliefs.
- Self-talk is the dialogue I have with myself to define my experiences and perceptions. This self-talk is generally influenced by my emotions and forms my beliefs. Beliefs are also formed by the words others speak to me and about me.

Over the course of my life, a number of experiences combined to create the deep negative beliefs about myself listed at the opening of this Dare. These negative beliefs unconsciously controlled my life. The fear of having these negative beliefs validated over and over again kept me from going after my dreams, from feeling confident and experiencing happiness and peace. I felt all this potential inside of me but I was so afraid of judgment and failure, so afraid to live, so afraid to show the world who I was because I knew, without a doubt, that I was flawed and others would see it and say "You're right, you're a loser." And I wouldn't be able to handle that. It would be too painful. So I stayed "safe" in my negative beliefs, choosing not to add to them.

Over the years of my healing journey, I slowly confronted my fears and my pain in small, safe ways until I was strong enough to face it in a more courageous and risky way. That risky way was competing in a beauty pageant. Where else could I be forced to confront my beliefs about my beauty, my worthiness and my fear of judgment head on? This experience put me face to face emotionally, mentally and physically with my beliefs and perceptions. I had to evaluate, examine and redefine them or I knew I would walk out on that stage and fail for sure. And I didn't want that.

As I've stated before, I'm not advocating beauty pageant participation. What I'm advocating is the challenge of looking at your beliefs and determining if maybe, just maybe, you have a few that are actually lies. You'll know they're lies if they steal your personal power, keep you limited, stagnant and unable to move forward in positive ways. They keep you "safe."

Unless we are willing to look at our beliefs and question their validity, we will remain where we are. That's why change is so hard. Anything that challenges our beliefs makes us feel unsafe and we don't want to feel unsafe. We might start moving forward with a goal or self-improvement project but then that unsafe feeling sets in and pulls us back again. Forward movement is a process of learning to trust uncertainty. New beliefs are scary. What if I really am beautiful? What if I really am lovable? What if I really am meant to be happy? What would that mean for me? What if I fully embraced who I am? What will be required then? And what if I can't do what is required?

It all comes down to choosing faith or fear. And it's a process that starts with the awareness and examination of our beliefs.

Today's Dare
I dare you to consider that some of your negative beliefs might actually be lies.
In addition . . .

I dare you to examine your thoughts and speech for negative beliefs about yourself. Journal about the validity of one specific thought or negative belief. Is it really true? How do you know? From where did this belief originate? What if the opposite of this belief is true? What will that mean for you? Does fear surface in connection with this belief? Does fear surface with the thought of the opposite potential belief? In other words, if "I am stupid" is my negative belief, do I feel fear if I consider the opposite belief "I am intelligent"? If so, why? Examining beliefs for truth is powerful. Like other tools, it introduces choice into the mix. Remember, the ability to choose is power.

Dare 11: Belief Hunt on Beauty

"For those who believe, no proof is necessary. For those who don't believe, no proof is possible."
~Stuart Chase

"You can have anything you want if you will give up the belief that you can't have it."
~Dr. Robert Anthony

    When I first committed to competing in a pageant, I was immediately confronted by my beliefs about beauty. I believed that a person needed to be "model beautiful" in every way to compete in a pageant and do well. In some pageant systems, there definitely is more of an emphasis on physical beauty, but this "model beauty" belief I held was largely my own and created great conflict within me because I felt I didn't belong in that group of beautiful women. However, the more I came to know the women with whom I competed, and the more I interacted with them, the more I came to understand what true beauty and feminine power looks like. There is no predefined shape or mold. Beauty is expressed in a unique combination of qualities, attributes and traits that varies with each individual. Every woman who competed in that pageant with me was indeed beautiful, but each woman conveyed her specific form of beauty in her own way, and it wasn't all physically based. It was the whole package, the entire presence that made each woman beautiful.

    I grew to appreciate the qualities these women possessed. They inspired me with the desire to be better. That is, until two weeks before the competition, when I was suddenly seized by insecurities and comparisons that buckled my budding confidence and admiration. I struggled from that point on until pageant night. Unfortunately, my fears about "not being enough" were validated when I failed to make the top ten finalists. It was quite a blow and motivated me to further examine my beliefs about beauty. I felt great conflict as I struggled to resolve my feelings of unworthiness as a pageant "loser" in contrast to the new beliefs I had been forming about what makes someone beautiful and a "winner."

Several weeks after the competition was over, each participant received a spreadsheet from the judges showing their scores and placement in each category of the competition. This information was enormously helpful in aiding my understanding that my self-judgments were severe and that I was actually a worthy competitor. By seeing the results and watching the video, I realized it wasn't necessarily a lack of beauty that kept me from reaching my goal of making the top ten. Rather, it was my overall performance and lack of confidence that showed on stage.

About a week after the pageant, there was a going away party for the director, who was moving out of state. As I visited with my former competitors at this party, and without the pressure of competition in the air, I discovered some amazing consistencies between the women I viewed as the most powerful and successful. I discovered they were manifesting the desires of their hearts, and if I wanted to be like them I simply needed to find a way to access and manifest that power in myself. What a great secret to understand! If I just developed and applied a few simple techniques, many of which you are learning in this book, I could be just as confident and accomplished as them!

As I began to explore this idea and look beyond rigid beliefs and indoctrination about beauty, I began to see it in a new light. I saw it as something that begins on the inside and resonates to the exterior, something that can be acquired rather than merely granted at birth by a genetic lottery. I began to consider, and even dared to believe, that I could be beautiful, truly beautiful.

There is so much beauty everywhere, if we have eyes to see it, and most of it is not physically based. A cultural paradigm shift about beauty is long overdue, but it begins within each one of us. What is your paradigm about beauty? Is it limited? Is it time for a new belief about who you are and what you look like?

Today's Dare

I dare you to consider the following truth:
YOU ARE BEAUTIFUL.
In addition . . .

Go on a belief hunt about beauty. Ask yourself some questions and journal your answers. What is your definition of beauty? What does that definition mean to you? What standards do you hold yourself to in order to label yourself as beautiful? Did you create your definition of beauty? Or did it come from other sources such as media, culture, peers, or family? Is what you wrote about beauty true? How do you know? Are you open to considering that there may be other definitions just as valid as your own?

Dare 12: Drug of Choice

"Self-acceptance comes from meeting life's challenges vigorously. Don't numb yourself to your trials and difficulties, nor build mental walls to exclude pain from your life. You will find peace not by trying to escape your problems, but by confronting them courageously. You will find peace not in denial, but in victory."
~J. Donald Walters

Right around the time I crashed emotionally and decided that I hated myself, I was sitting in my big chair-and-a-half reading . . . again. I stopped for a minute. My head felt fuzzy. I put my book down and cleaned the kitchen. Later, I took some time to write in my journal and consider my reading habits. I was checking out 30 books a week from the library and buying many others on a regular basis. I was cramming my head so full of information that I didn't have time to think about anything else but what I was reading. The problem was that I had all this disconnected information running amuck in my brain for so long that I literally *felt* disconnected. I discovered, or rather finally admitted, that reading had become my "drug of choice."

Anything we use to numb our emotions can become a "drug of choice." For some, it is literally drugs, prescription or recreational. For others, it may be television, music, or food. Even sports, exercise and other healthy activities can become "drugs of choice" when we use them beyond the point of moderation to obscure or avoid emotions or emotional pain.

How do you know if you have a drug of choice? First, you have to be open to the idea that you might indeed have one. Next, you have to observe and be aware of your behavior and tendencies. Then, if there is a problem, you have to address it.

Behaviors that steal personal power have motivations behind them that render us weak. Those motivations are generally based on the avoidance of pain. Motivations are the fuel behind behavior. No fuel, no movement. But as long as motivation exists, so does the potential to develop or practice addictions of any kind, at any level. I'm not talking about peer-motivated behaviors, or genetic tendencies and family predispositions to substances. Our purpose here is to identify whether you have a "drug of choice" in connection to emotional pain. If your desire to stuff and ignore emotional pain is strong enough, then you will find a way to cope that is both acceptable to your conscience and effective in numbing your pain. This is where a drug of choice emerges. It really depends on who you are as to how your drug of choice manifests, but everyone is susceptible to having one.

That said, individuals suffering from clinical conditions such as anxiety or depression (or other medical or psychological conditions) need not judge themselves because they must take medication to manage their condition. The drug of choice I am talking about is more an addictive action to mask pain, so keep that in mind as you consider these things.

Today's Dare
I dare you to acknowledge that we are a culture of addiction and pain numbing, and that you are susceptible to these behaviors as a member of that culture. No addiction can be healed that is not recognized or acknowledged.
In addition . . .

I dare you to consider and journal whether or not you have a "drug of choice," a preferred coping mechanism for dealing with emotional pain. If so, have you taken it to the extreme? Or is it still within "healthy" boundaries? Consider your motivations behind the behavior. What types of events or circumstances trigger you turning to that particular "drug"? If you do have a "drug of choice," how badly is it affecting you? If you are not progressing it is affecting you. What can you do to change that behavior to become a stronger individual?

Dare 13: Belief Hunt on Worthiness

"To have that sense of one's intrinsic worth which constitutes self-respect is potentially to have everything: the ability to discriminate, to love and to remain indifferent."
~Joan Didion

"In every aspect of our lives, we are always asking ourselves, How am I of value? What is my worth? Yet I believe that worthiness is our birthright."
~Oprah Winfrey

It was such a weird dream, so many strange symbols. The most prominent elements were the pink and black squares on the floor, more black ones than pink ones. I knew this dream was significant and needed to be analyzed, so I broke out my favorite dream dictionary and my journal and started to work.

First, I wrote a summary of my dream, followed by the specific details and their definitions. Then I went back through the dream again with the new understanding of what the dream symbols meant and WOW! I had one of the biggest epiphanies of my life! I uncovered an immensely negative belief of which only my subconscious mind was aware until that moment. The method of delivery my subconscious chose to communicate this invaluable information to me was a dream. Who knows if my subconscious had tried to deliver it in other ways? I obviously had not listened. But at this time in my life, I needed to understand this belief I held or I would not be able to progress. This belief underscored EVERYTHING in my life. I believed the following:

I was created to suffer.

That's a pretty heavy and sabotaging belief. What does a person's life look like who believes something like this? Pretty normal and unremarkable from the outside. On the inside? Miserable. Once I understood this belief,

I was able to see how it manifested in my life. I tended to make decisions based on the desires of others and never on my own. I felt like I always had to "give in" and sacrifice, suffer. It also held me back from making choices that would bring me success or happiness and kept me paralyzed in situations that were sucking the life out of me. Even in matters of religion (where I felt immovable), I still applied this belief. In fact, I used religion as my justification for suffering, telling myself it was required. On some level, I suppose I even thought it noble to suffer for others. My perceptions on suffering were distorted, to say the least.

One day I saw a quote by Gordon B. Hinckley, former President of the Church of Jesus Christ of Latter-day Saints. It said, "Life is to be enjoyed, not just endured." Wow. I was completely missing out. I was enduring, but that was it. No joy, just suffering and endurance of suffering, and feeling like I deserved it.

Understanding that I had beliefs that pegged me as unworthy of happiness empowered me to realize that I could make choices based on what I wanted, that I wasn't required to suffer to be worthy of living. When I make choices now, I consider what is best for me and others. I weigh *all* the options, consider them in my heart and mind, and then decide. Suffering no longer rules my life. Sure, I will still suffer sometimes for various reasons, but it won't be because I believe I deserve it and am required to live a life of suffering. We are not meant for suffering, but for joy.

Today's Dare

I dare you to consider that you might just have major beliefs that keep you feeling like you are not worthy of love, joy, success, wealth or anything else good in life.
In addition . . .

I dare you to think and journal about your beliefs in regards to personal worthiness. Do you feel worthy of love? Belonging? Having? Asking? Receiving?

Don't know what your deepest beliefs are? Consider dream interpretation as an option for uncovering those secrets your subconscious mind holds. All the answers about you that you'll ever need are within you. In fact, I dare you to try dream interpretation at least once.

Dare 14: Healing and Time

"Healing is a matter of time, but it is sometimes also a matter of opportunity."
~Hippocrates

When I talk about healing, I am talking about positive life changes—changes in beliefs which ultimately change your experience of life. This is healing. It is a return to the wholeness you experienced as a newborn baby, before life told you what to believe.

One of the most beautiful aspects of this type of healing is that you get to heal at your own rate! You control that rate by managing your pain. What I mean is you won't allow yourself to feel any more pain than you are ready to process and therefore you move only at a rate at which you can handle. Most of us get stuck in our pain because instead of managing it, we numb it. There is a difference. Managing pain means pushing through it. Numbing pain means avoidance.

My mom recently had a total knee replacement. Yes, they gave her painkillers to numb the pain, but they also gave her an extensive regimen of exercises and rules to follow to manage and heal her pain. I watched her meticulously obey all of the instructions the doctors, nurses and physical therapists gave her to help her knee heal properly. She only took as much painkiller as necessary, allowing herself to endure as much pain as possible, so as not to depend upon the drugs too much. She did all the exercises required, even though they were painful, and followed all the rules. When she went to her two-week checkup, the doctors were amazed at her rate of healing! Because she controlled her use of pain-numbing medications and pushed forward through pain with perseverance, she had miraculous results.

My point here is not to instruct you in physical healing, but to use my mom's experience to illustrate how pushing through discomfort, rather than numbing it, led her to rapid and successful healing.

We have the same opportunity with healing beliefs, or changing our lives. We can numb life, or we can push through discomfort and experience change. We can listen to the guidance of our spirit, emotions, and even professionals, and apply their wisdom or we can stay stuck.

Trust your inner wisdom; listen to your heart, your body, your mind and especially, your spirit. They hold great wisdom. Get help when you need it. But continue onward. It will be so worth the freedom you will experience in the end.

The butterfly has become one of my favorite symbols. It goes through immense pain to take on its light and beautiful wings. It is a symbol of successful transformation brought about through pain and struggle. I love the butterfly for all her humility, endurance and courage. How wonderful that we all possess these qualities, can call upon them, and develop them through our individual journeys!

Today's Dare
I dare you to remember always that healing takes time, but that timeline is negotiable according to your faith and courage to face issues head on.
In addition . . .

I dare you to open up to the pain of transformation. I dare you to be like the butterfly and secure your wings. I dare you to write in your journal about the possibilities that could occur for you if your particular pain were healed. What would that mean for you? What would your life look like? Do you foresee your "healing journey" taking a long time? Why? What stands in your way? What would you do with your "wings" if you had them? What does your heart tell you about pacing? Have you uncovered any hidden fears about healing and change while considering these things?

Dare 15: I AM

"Knowledge is two-fold, and consists not only in an affirmation of what is true, but in the negation of that which is false."
~Charles Caleb Colton

"You will be a failure, until you impress the subconscious with the conviction you are a success. This is done by making an affirmation which 'clicks.' "
~Florence Scovel Shinn

You don't have to be religious to appreciate the magnitude of what I'm about to share with you.

In the Bible, at John 1:1, we are told that "In the beginning was the Word, and the Word was with God, and the Word *was* God."

This says something fascinating about the power of words. At the very beginning of everything, the Word existed. And it was so powerful that the world was created by it.

Here's another example from Christian scripture. In Exodus, Chapter 3, we read the story of Moses' visit with God, who appeared to him in a burning bush. During their conversation, Moses asks God what his name is. God replies "I AM."

It's one thing to realize that words are associated with power. Period. But if you consider that the specific words "I AM" are associated with God's name, then we're talking serious power. How many times a day do you use the words "I AM"? What descriptions are you attaching to those words? Do you realize that when you say "I AM so stupid" that you are attaching major power to that statement? Any word you attach to an I AM statement is incredibly powerful because it is attached to the power of God.

Affirmations are positive I AM statements. One of the reasons they work is because of this powerful connection to God. But the other reason they work is this . . .

Let's say you have the belief "I AM ugly." When you first state a counter affirmation like "I AM beautiful," your mind won't really believe it. This creates an imbalance within you. Your mind says, "Wait a minute. That's not true. I better fix this." If you continue to repeat the positive statement on a regular basis, your mind will seek to become congruent with the new statement. You can't embrace both beliefs at the same time. Your mind must choose one or the other. Energy is directed where your focus lies. Repeating a positive affirmation trains your mind in the way you WANT and desire to feel, and focuses energy on your efforts.

When I was first introduced to affirmations, I thought they were a bunch of garbage. I felt dumb writing these "lies" about myself and even dumber speaking them. But as I persisted, I quickly got over the discomfort and found them to be empowering.

In clarification, affirmations are not attempts to convince yourself that you are not struggling, or to deny the existence of problems. Rather, affirmations are validations of positive attributes you want to embody, and the truth beneath the lies you tell yourself and believe. Reciting affirmations that deny issues like "I have no problems" is a lie and will always be met with failure. Everybody has problems. You will continue to have problems arise until the day you die. A better way to phrase that would be "I excel at solving problems when they arise." Or "I AM an excellent problem solver." Make sure your affirmations are phrased for success so that you don't self-sabotage.

I highly recommend using this powerful tool on your journey toward loving yourself.

Today's Dare
If you don't already, I dare you to open up to the idea of creating and reciting affirmations.
In addition . . .

Write a list of 10 affirmations that will empower you to develop more self-love, more confidence and more personal power. Write these in your journal and recite them daily. Make it a part of your morning and/or evening routine. Notice how it gets easier over time to speak these wonderful things about yourself. As a double dare, I challenge you to take your list to the mirror, look right in your eyes and say each affirmation with conviction.

Dare 16: Journaling

"I am enamored of my journal."
~Sir Walter Scott

"Journal writing is a voyage to the interior"
~Christina Baldwin

During the first week of *The Love Yourself Dare*, we began recording physical sensations in our portable journal, like water intake, exercise frequency, and sleep habits. Now is the time to take out your journal and see if you can recognize any patterns emerging in what you have recorded? Are you getting enough water each day? Enough sleep? Enough exercise? These are basic power actions of which you should be aware. If you find that you are negligent in any of these areas may I suggest—no, I dare you—to commit to creating habits of personal power in these areas. You may find a mentor, life coach or personal trainer helpful. Only you will know the best way to implement these healthy habits into your routine. If you find yourself making excuses about any specific area, then you'll know you've hit on an area of potential power for you, a place of fear that is being covered by excuses. I dare you to take the steps to address it.

Journals play an important part in documenting that which can empower you. Had you not recorded the information above in your journal, you may not have seen your lifestyle choices and patterns clearly. This knowledge gives you power to make new choices in connection with the information recorded. Maybe you weren't aware that you were only getting 1-2 glasses of water per day. Increasing that amount will help improve so many important body functions that you won't be able to help but reap positive benefits from that one simple act alone. Likewise, maybe you weren't aware that you were consistently only getting six hours of sleep but would really excel if you got seven or eight. Knowledge is power.

In addition, journaling about the dares we do daily, and journaling about personal thoughts, feelings and problems allows you to release a lot of the clutter in your mind and body. Also, journaling allows you to validate what you are experiencing. I used to have someone in my life always telling me I was "too sensitive," or "ridiculous," and that my feelings weren't justified and my perceptions were off. I discovered my journal was a safe place where I could express any and every feeling, thought, perception and "sensitivity" without fear of judgment or ridicule. A journal is more than a tool—it is the perfect, trustworthy friend.

Today's Dare

I dare you to consider that a journal could be a powerful tool for you. In addition . . .

I dare you to take out your journal and write a stream-of-consciousness entry. Just write for 5 to 10 minutes, or for two to three pages without stopping. If you run out of things to write, just write "I don't know what to write" over and over until something comes up. Doing this exercise will rid you of a lot of accumulated mental and emotional chatter. It will promote clarity and stillness within you. If you do this exercise first thing in the morning, you will generally find your day to be less stressful. Try it, I dare you.

Dare 17: Personality Profile

*"Personality is the glitter that sends your little gleam across the footlights
And the orchestra pit into that big black space where the audience is."*
~Mae West

*"I hold that a strongly marked personality can influence descendants
for generations."*
~Beatrix Potter

I am a blue. No, a yellow. No, a white. Wait, what am I?

Most people are familiar with *The Color Code* by Dr. Taylor Hartman. It's a great basic personality profile that provides understanding about the core make up of a person's personality. If you say, "You're such a white," most people will know what you mean. However, in the search for deep self-knowledge, I have found this book to be lacking. For the serious seeker of self, I suggest a number of personality profiles rather than just one. I recommend starting with *The Color Code* to get a general idea of core personality type, and build on that. Don't take it as gospel. Each personality profile you take will shed light on new aspects of yourself and broaden your understanding of self.

Here is the list I suggest:

- *The Color Code*, Dr. Taylor Hartman
- *Please Understand Me II* (The Keirsey Temperament sorter), David Keirsey and Marilyn Bates
- *Wired That Way*, Dr. Marita Littauer. I love this book. It is written from a Christian perspective (which may not be your thing) but the information in it is SO useful. It is the only personality book I have found that addresses the concept of "masking." This was essential in uncovering my true personality type. As I took these profiles, I consistently came up with scores that indicated I was equal between two

personality types. This is supposedly impossible, but no matter how I approached the tests the results always came out the same—a split between two. Then I learned about masking. Masking is a coping tool that people use when they have experienced painful or abusive relationships. They cover up the core personality and compensate to stay "safe." Once I learned this concept, I was free to really see myself for who I am. Again, this is the only book I've come across that describes this important concept.

- *The Enneagram.* You can find these tests Online or in books and there are a lot of them. They are educational as well. In addition to defining core personality strengths, they suggest ways to balance the negative aspects of personality. Good stuff.

There are other books on personality, but these should get you started. In addition, numerology profiles can also provide added insight into your personality. There are several free Online. Understanding how you operate, your tendencies and preferences is an empowering thing. This search also helps you understand other people too. We don't come with an instruction manual when we are born. The more you know about yourself and others, the greater advantage you have in life. Those who don't make the effort to gain valuable self-knowledge are left to drift and struggle and wonder.

Today's Dare

I dare you to acquire one of the above books from a library or bookstore and take a profile. What did you learn about yourself that you didn't already know? Remember that these are general profiles. You will not meet every description summarized within the book's pages. Because of spiritual, character and value differences in individuals, you can't possibly fit every detail of a personality type. Enjoy the process of self-discovery.

Dare 18: Talent and Gift Inventory

*"Use what talents you possess; the woods would be very silent
If no birds sang there except those that sang best."*
~Henry Van Dyke

*"We are not in a position in which we have nothing to work with.
We already have capacities, talents, directions, missions,
callings."*
~Abraham Maslow

One of the fun parts of learning to love yourself is coming to understand your strengths and gifts. When you figure out where you excel, and how you can use what you have to bless the world in truly unique ways, it's exciting! Your gifts and passions combine to create a life vision, a purpose for your life that is larger than yourself alone. This is great stuff! It's what gives life meaning and makes it all worthwhile. When you are living your purpose each day, life is a wonderful journey!

When people consider talents, they tend to think of the arts, crafts or sports—visual or physical gifts. I hear people say, "I don't have any talents" because their gifts don't fit into these categories. That's exactly why I use the word gifts. A gift is anything you've been blessed with to which you are naturally inclined, no matter the level of development. One of my gifts is the ability to express love through words of appreciation or compliments without reservation. It's something that comes easily and naturally to me. I consider it a gift because I have seen how it positively affects others even though it might not be considered a talent per se.

As you consider what you are good at think broader than the concrete. I write songs, I dance, I sing, I'm an artist, I'm a writer—these are some of my concrete talents. Some of my abstract gifts are the gifts of compassion and empathy, faith, creativity, sensitivity, versatility, directness, and depth. Some of these don't seem like obvious gifts. I mean, how is depth or directness a gift? Depth allows me to reach further into relationships and education, to feel meaning in my life and then share that with others. Directness allows me to get straight to the point, saving me and others time and drama. Think outside the box when thinking of gifts.

Today's Dare
I dare you to acknowledge that you have more gifts and talents than you currently recognize.
In addition . . .

I dare you to list an inventory of talents and gifts you possess. Continue to add to this list every time you discover another positive trait about yourself that you regularly exemplify. This is a gift. This unique combination of attributes and powers are yours and yours alone. No one else has this exact combination of gifts and talents. You can use these gifts to not only change your life, but to positively influence the lives of others. But first you must be aware of what they are. Be generous in your evaluation, there are no prizes for modesty here. Be bold! Be willing to see the amazing things about yourself that are there inside of you. I dare you!

Dare 19: Alignment

"When you examine the lives of the most influential people who have ever walked among us, you discover one thread that winds through them all. They have been aligned first with their spiritual nature and only then with their physical selves."
~Albert Einstein

The dictionary defines alignment in the following ways:
1. To arrange in a straight line.
2. To bring into cooperation or agreement with something.

I like to think of alignment as two or more things coming together and overlapping entirely, or becoming One.

Alignment is such an important aspect in loving yourself. Alignment is the honoring of self, God and purpose. It is applied respect that gives attention to, and acknowledges, the importance of three key areas of power.

God

First, and most importantly, you have to align yourself with God, or a Higher Power. To believe in something greater than oneself is to access a whole host of powers beyond the understanding. Believing in something greater than oneself is to ignite the flame of hope and the capacity for miracles in life.

To align with God, or a Higher Power, requires that you have a conscious understanding of your beliefs and that you live them.

Respecting and honoring this Higher Power is a sign of personal humility, which is a position of power, and fosters self-love. It is only when we are humble enough to see our weaknesses and allow them to exist that we can move to a position of power and strength regarding them.

Personal Values

Personal values are our character foundation and what we automatically base our actions on. If you don't know what your personal values are, I suggest you take the time to discover them. I keep a list of my top ten personal values visible as a reminder of what is truly important in my life. If an opportunity manifests in my life that doesn't support these values at the level I am currently living them, or above, then I know it's not an opportunity I should take.

My personal values are the things with which I try to align my actions; they are the things I cherish most. For example, love is one of my highest values. When I live in a way that is not congruent with the love I usually feel, I fall out of alignment with myself and my Higher Power. I'm not suggesting infallible consistency here. That's impossible. Let me illustrate what I mean.

My natural state is to love everyone I meet. Sometimes I meet a person against whom I feel resistance. This is an unnatural state for me and I immediately feel out of alignment. To bring myself back into alignment, I have to ask myself some questions to discover the source of that resistance. Sometimes it's merely a personality clash, other times fear, or sometimes even envy. At other times, the resistance comes from my intuition and tells me that this person is not a healthy association for me. Once I know the reason for the resistance, I can honor my understanding in the way it needs to be honored and become realigned. Realignment doesn't mean forcing myself into an uncomfortable association. It is honoring my highest good. Sometimes that means loving a person and myself enough to NOT become associated with them. It's a process of understanding the self and what you need to feel congruent and whole.

Another illustration is someone who never lies, but then tells a "little white lie" and feels guilty. That guilty feeling is an indicator that you are out of alignment with your usual level of integrity. However, you also have to be aware that guilt is tricky and complicated. You can feel guilt for things you shouldn't as a way to keep yourself "safe" or "protected." You have to investigate and understand the source of your guilt. Is it an issue of alignment, or something else?

To discover your top ten values write a list of the things to which you are most drawn that are the most important to you on a daily basis. What are the things that make you furious when someone violates them? Do you absolutely hate conflict? Then peace is probably one of your values. Do you find yourself always creating something? Then creativity or expression is probably one of your values. Integrity encompasses many values, as does love. It's worth knowing what you value so you can measure whether or not you are aligned in your life.

Desires

Aligning with my desires was something that took me awhile to get. I could easily understand how to align with God and my values, but aligning with my true desires was hard for me. It was scary. It suggested to me responsibility that I wasn't sure I had the confidence or capacity to fulfill. I masked my true desires and was confused about what I wanted in life because of fear. My greatest dreams and desires seemed too big, too unrealistic, and too unlikely for someone like me, so I tried to find realistic dreams and settle for lesser desires. I quickly became confused and lost direction and purpose in my life. I have since learned that confusion is simply the truth obscured by an inability to listen to the heart. In other words, when I feel confusion about something, it's usually because I already know the answer and I'm not willing to admit or accept it.

You aren't fully aligned with God or with your values if you are not aligned with your desires because your good desires are generally an extension of your values and are usually supported by God. They are also a significant part of who you are. To deny or hush good desires is to dishonor yourself. Desires are placed within you for a reason. There are lessons to be learned, skills to be gained, ways to serve and bless others as you bring these desires to life. To align with your desires is to align all three points of power.

Truth

Truth touches all three points of alignment—the truth on which you base your Higher Power beliefs, the truth on which you base your personal values, and the truth on which you base your desires. If any of these areas are based on distorted truths, it will usually show up in the type of results you are getting. If you seem to be stuck or confused a lot, it's time to look at the "truths" you hold in relation to your worthiness, capability or possibility. Examine your beliefs about these things to determine whether your "truth" is distorted.

If you "always screw up," perhaps it is time to reevaluate that belief. Yes, you may be able to find lots of "proof" that supports that statement, but it doesn't mean it's true. It is merely what you choose to believe. Perhaps it's time for a more empowering belief like, "I always succeed."

In conclusion, alignment is power. To bring your values, Higher Power, and desires all into agreement is the recipe for miracles in your life. It is the path to peace and joy. When a person is congruent in these three ways, based on the truth, they will feel confident, directed and powerful.

Today's Dare

I dare you to consider and journal about these three points of alignment. Are you out of alignment in any of these areas? Are you connecting with and trying to live in accordance to your beliefs regarding your God, or your Higher Power? Are you living in accordance with your highest values? Do you even know what those values are? If not, take a few minutes to discover those values. Are you living in accordance with your greatest desires? Even the ones that seem impossible or scary? Or are you denying those desires because a lack of faith in yourself or God? Consider small ways in which you can improve and embrace these things more fully.

Dare 20: Stillness

"Stillness of person and steadiness of features are signal marks of good breeding"
~Oliver Wendell Holmes

"In the midst of movement and chaos, keep stillness inside of you."
~Deepak Chopra

    The body is the companion to the spirit; therefore it's our responsibility to learn how our spirits communicate through our bodies. As I come to understand how my body specifically communicates to my spirit and vice versa, I realize I can discern problems in my life much more quickly.

    Everything in our lives is symbolic. Our spiritual bodies duplicate our physical bodies. If we understand our physical anatomy and physiology, it will teach us about our spiritual anatomy and physiology, and how we can keep our spirits and bodies pure and operating optimally.

    At one point in my life, I made it a regular habit to create stillness in my life. I took time on a daily basis to be still in body and quiet in mind, to focus on relaxation and feeling whole and healed emotionally. Sometimes, I would visualize specific things, other times I would simply listen to my body or my heart and allow it to be "heard." But every day I would be still. When I took a trip to Maui a few years ago, I connected with a greater, higher sense of stillness and peace than I have ever felt before or since. Stillness in nature facilitates tremendous peace.

    As women we are so busy, fragmented into a thousand pieces and directions every day. We need regular stillness in our lives, a specific time to get in touch with who we are and what we feel. Stillness breeds clarity, which in turn breeds confidence, personal power and peace.

    Stillness is a form of grounding. Grounding is imperative for personal power and confidence. What is grounding? Grounding is the process of re-connecting yourself to your foundation, your Center. Grounding is a conscious re-aligning with your highest values, God, intentions and desires (like we discussed in Dare 19). Grounding can be achieved in a number of ways. For example, kneading bread, digging in the garden, walking in nature—anything that connects you to the earth and your roots, while centering you and calming you is grounding. When done consciously, it's a very powerful practice.

It is important to have both stillness and grounding activities in your life on a regular basis. If you want to hear your heart, you must be still and quiet. If you want to connect to your Source and realign your busy body and busy mind, you have to ground.

Today's Dare

Take a few moments out of your day to be still. Journal about what happens when you are purposefully still. Do you feel sensations in your body that you weren't aware of before? What are they telling you? That you're stressed? Tired? Sore? Do you feel emotions you hadn't noticed because of your daily pace or noise in your life? What else do you notice in stillness? Stillness does not have to be a focused meditation. At this point, just try to still your body and mind for 5 minutes and record what you observe.

If this seems too difficult, try a conscious grounding activity to help quiet yourself first. Take a walk without your phone or mp3 player, or sit in a lawn chair and do nothing, or pull weeds, just connect with nature in some way. Then try 5 minutes of stillness. Record your experience.

Dare 21: Nutrition

"The greatest wealth is health."
~Unknown

"If you don't take care of your body, where are you going to live?"
~Unknown

We've been doing a lot of internal observation. I'd like to focus for a few days on some physical ways to love yourself.

Today, we're going to look at nutrition. I'm not a nutritionist, so I'm not going to provide dietary suggestions on the topic. There are plenty of good books on the subject by qualified professionals, as well as recommendations you can get from your doctor or other health professional. What I do suggest is that you record everything you eat for the next several days in your journal to get a good representation of your current diet.

As I've stated before, we increase or decrease our vibrational frequency (energy level) by the things we ingest into our bodies. What we eat profoundly affects our health and well-being, even our mental and emotional functioning. If your general health is struggling, it will be very difficult to address loving yourself on a mental and emotional level, which is where true self-love is acquired. Still, the physical aspect is huge, and directly intertwined with the other two in the process of loving yourself. We must address all aspects to feel fabulous, confident and centered. I can't stress enough how important it is to begin showing love for yourself by honoring your physical body and its nutritional needs.

Today's Dare

For the next several days write down everything you eat. Look at your diet. Is it healthy? Are you getting the good foods that you need? Or is your diet full of carbohydrates, fats and processed foods? Can you begin making a shift toward honoring your body through good nutrition? What is one thing you can begin doing today? Try cutting your intake of sugar to half, or drinking one less soda. You decide, but love your body by fueling it with good foods. You will literally feel the difference within.

Dare 22: Stress Management

"At times of great stress it is especially necessary to achieve a complete freeing of the muscles."
~Konstantin Stanislavsky

"The greatest weapon against stress is our ability to choose one thought over another."
~William James

    Life constantly creates stress. In addition to daily challenges, the process of learning to love yourself can create additional stress because it brings us face to face with uncomfortable feelings associated with changing behavior.
    Stress has many negative effects on our bodies. The following are some excerpts from an article by The American Psychological Association (http://www.apa.org/monitor/julaug02/experts.aspx):

- A summary of 37 studies shows that stress management and life-style-change programs can help reduce the number of deaths from heart disease by 34%.
- Studies show that stress can be a factor in triggering heart disease, and the severity can be increased when combined with other risk factors, such as a poor diet and smoking.
- Many people shy away from adopting healthier lifestyles because of the difficulty and stress involved in changing behavior.

    Stress can wreak havoc in our lives. In 2010, I spent six consecutive months battling throat infection after throat infection, severe fatigue and back pain. Medical tests showed nothing wrong with me. The doctor said it was stress induced. The adrenals can get fatigued from too much stress and leave our bodies weak and unable to resist illness.

Prior to the time I fell ill, I regularly included stress-reducing activities in my life on a daily basis, but the new year brought a new level of stress and those healthy habits quickly succumbed to illness and I stopped doing them. Whenever I incorporate stress-reducing activities into my life I feel good. I feel empowered and better able to cope with problems that come my way. I feel confident and I also remain healthier.

Here are a few suggestions to help manage stress:
- **Exercise:** I find exercise to be my number one stress fighter. If I exercise with the intention of releasing stress, I generally work harder while I'm doing it and feel amazing when I'm done. You can exercise without intention, but when you add an intention, a focus, to your workout, it makes it more productive.
- **Deep Relaxation:** The most effective relaxation method I've found for myself is to lie on the ground (or bed) on my back and breathe deeply. I start by focusing on my head and let it "sink" into the earth as I exhale. Then I move to my shoulders, down my arms and torso, etc. down to my feet. I picture the tension draining out of me and into the earth. This works really well for releasing tension from the muscles. This can be done sitting too, if you have back problems.
- **Meditation:** You can use guided meditations or you can create your own. A meditation is simply a focused thought process in a state of stillness. I like to lie on my back and visualize pure, white light entering every part of my being and filling me with energy that heals. Look for or create meditations that target your specific needs.
- **Grounding and Stillness:** These help facilitate stress management, as we stated in Day 20.
- **Essential Oils**: I love pure therapeutic grade essential oils. I use these to help facilitate emotional release and to support health issues that arise from time to time. The molecules from essential oils, when inhaled, pass the blood-brain barrier and have a great positive effect on moods and emotions.
- **Nature:** Getting out in nature, without a phone or mp3 player, and just enjoying the beauties of the earth can bring great peace and feelings of gratitude to life, which in turn helps reduce stress. If you can get out and enjoy nature, listen to the sounds, take in the beauties that surround you and feel the breeze, it can be very relaxing and rejuvenating.
- **Music:** Music has a great affect on our moods and emotions. We

generally listen to that which resonates with us at the moment. For example, if we are in love, we tend to listen to love songs. If we are sad, we listen to sad songs. We can also use music to change our moods. Listening to music you know makes you feel good, or relaxed, when you're not feeling that way and it can help promote the change you wish to feel within yourself.

- **Gratitude:** It is said that gratitude is the highest vibration that exists in the emotional world. There is nothing like feeling pure gratitude to chase stress away.

Recently, while struggling with some pretty big stresses, a dear friend taught me a profound and simple truth. He said:

Stress is choice.

Stress is also an automatic reaction to specific stimuli. Once aware of habitual action in response to specific stimuli, stress really does become a choice. I don't want stress to have power over my life. I choose freedom.

Today's Dare

Pick one stress reduction method and incorporate it into your routine on a regular basis.

Dare 23: Safety and Boundaries

"The purpose of having boundaries is to protect and take care of ourselves. We need to be able to tell other people when they are acting in ways that are not acceptable to us. A first step is starting to know that we have a right to protect and defend ourselves. That we have not only the right, but the duty to take responsibility for how we allow others to treat us."
~Robert Burney

If you're familiar with psychology you probably know about Maslow's Hierarchy of Needs. Here is some basic information taken from a website on this topic (http://www.simplypsychology.org/maslow.html):

"Maslow described self-actualized people as those who were fulfilled and doing all they were capable of. Maslow identified 15 characteristics of a self-actualized person. It is not necessary to display all 15 characteristics to become self-actualized, and not only self-actualized people will display them. Maslow did not equate self-actualization with perfection. Self-actualization merely involves achieving ones potential. Less than one percent of the population achieves self-actualization.

"Maslow (1970) presents a hierarchy of needs pyramid which can be divided into basic (or deficiency) needs (e.g. physiological, safety, love, and esteem) growth needs (cognitive, aesthetics and self-actualization). One must satisfy lower level basic needs before progressing on to meet higher level growth needs. Once these needs have been reasonably satisfied, one may be able to reach the highest level called self-actualization."

A few Dares ago, we briefly discussed the idea of meeting basic needs before attempting higher level change in the emotional realm. Most of us are getting our base-level physiological needs met, but many of us get stuck on the second level regarding safety needs. We may not be in any physical danger, but the fear of the unknown or the fear of getting hurt emotionally keeps us locked in place.

I spent countless years fearful of reprimands, chastisements, judgments and hurtful comments from others. Although I could give a measure of love and respect to other people, I couldn't give them to myself. I also couldn't live my dreams or reach any level of satisfying success because of these fears regarding safety.

I also struggled with boundary issues. Because I lost the essence of who I was to please another person, I had very few healthy boundaries. When we don't have boundaries we feel unsafe, which also keeps us stuck. In my past, I struggled with boundary issues because I had very little self-respect. Self-respect comes before confidence. You must have that foundation first.

How do you know if you're struggling with a boundary issue? Some clues are: If you are always compromising yourself, or feeling taken advantage of, or if you feel violated in some way. A book I checked out from the library called *Boundaries and Relationships* by Charles Whitfield, M.D. has excellent information on this very issue.

Today's Dare

Study a copy of Maslow's Hierarchy of Needs (you can find one Online through a Google images search). Are your basic needs being met? Are you struggling with any boundary issues? Can you pinpoint them? Where did they originate from? How can you create healthy boundaries for yourself? Are there any other needs not being met? Is your physical health in line? Are you treating any illnesses or conditions that should be treated? The more secure your foundation, the more power you have as you move up and down the pyramid throughout life.

Dare 24: Balance

"Everything in life, . . . has to have balance."
~*Donna Karan*

"I learned again that the mind-body-spirit connection has to be in balance."
~*Wynonna Judd*

Balance.

It's such an elusive thing. Here today, gone tomorrow.

Balance is slippery. It's not something you can ever count on consistently because each day brings change. Change in resources, change in responsibilities, change in circumstances.

One thing busy women seek is balance. We ask, "How do I manage it all?" Well first, you might want to consider the following question:

Do I need to manage it ALL? Is everything I'm doing *required*?

Really?

Balance is not perfection. Balance is not doing it all. Balance is a feeling of peace, a feeling that often eludes us. Why? Because we are approaching balance in the wrong way. We don't find balance by discovering some secret to managing our overstuffed lives. We find balance in moderation, the lack of extremes. We find balance as we do a manageable amount consistently over a period of time. We find balance as we prioritize. We find balance as we honor who we are at the core and love the self. We find balance when we do the things we know we should be doing instead of betraying ourselves by doing menial things that make us feel important because we can check them off our to-do list. Balance is doing the things that matter most. Balance is finding contentment in what you have to offer on any given day and letting the rest go.

Balance comes as we simplify. Simplification is really just a matter of making choices, shedding the unnecessary. Sometimes we fool ourselves into believing everything is necessary. What will really happen if your children aren't in three different lessons a week? Will you have failed as a parent? Really? Simplification, which leads to balance, is a process of asking questions and getting honest with ourselves about the answers.

Today's Dare

I dare you for the next day or two to get up a little early and write down everything you need to accomplish that day, or even better, do this the night before. Sit in stillness and look at your list. What does your heart tell you should be done first? Prioritize your day according to your highest values. Honor yourself by doing what needs to be done. Let the rest go. I'm not suggesting you be irresponsible in any way, but do those things that will bring you peace instead of everything you *think* you should be doing. If your heart says exercise, but you feel you have too much to do to fit that in, let something go, move it to another day, so that you can honor your heart. See how you feel when you do this. Do you feel more peaceful? Do you feel a greater sense of balance? Do you have more to offer others because you honored your needs? Write your experience in your journal.

Dare 25: Coloring Feelings

"It is still an unending source of surprise for me how a few scribbles on a blackboard
Or on a piece of paper can change the course of human affairs."
~Stanislaw Ulam

I learned a powerful, yet simple technique to release emotional garbage.

One of the biggest breakthroughs I had in relation to my self-worth and beauty was on my birthday. A friend stopped by and we talked. She is a facilitator for emotional release and taught me a powerful modality that day. She asked me to get a notebook and some crayons and color out what I was feeling, not in pictures, but with scribbles. Yes, it seems very juvenile, but I found this to be incredibly powerful. The picture that came out initially was green and gray, but as we got deeper into my feelings the scribbles turned heavily to black and red and then to almost all black.

I considered those pictures pretty ugly creations that definitely represented some deep, dark junk. With those emotions out on the page, I was then able to more clearly articulate what I was feeling underneath all the emotion. Scribbling feelings removes blocks to verbal expression.

I learned a powerful lesson that day. The best time to release and reprogram a negative belief is when you are right in the thick of the emotion. You can do this with affirmations (like we discussed in Dare 15). When you express an affirmation that rebukes negative beliefs, you are disrupting a pattern. If I say "I AM beautiful" loudly and with conviction when I am sobbing because I feel ugly, I create a break in that negative energy flow and combat the lie in the key moment when it will have the most effect.

Did you ever see *Ella Enchanted* with Anne Hathaway? In the moment of pure emotion, when she is holding the knife over Prince Char because she has been commanded under a curse to kill him, she summons the courage, through tears and intense emotional struggle, to command herself not to obey. Because of this, she is released from the curse, saving the Prince's life. It is much the same for us. It is hard to fight habits and beliefs. They are like a curse that keeps us captive and "obedient" to lies. If, in the moment of truth when we are feeling the negative emotion, we can summon the conviction to command ourselves to believe otherwise, we gain strength and a measure of power over our lives. Coloring out feelings can assist this process by releasing some of the emotions that keep us from accessing the words we need to speak.

I have used coloring feelings with my toddler. Right after my divorce, he was acting out with lots of anger. He wouldn't talk to me and I was concerned. I got out the crayons and drew faces representing each family member on a piece of paper. I said, "This is Mommy. What color do you think of when you think of Mommy?" He picked up a red crayon and scribbled all over the face I'd drawn on the page. I knew by the color choice that he was feeling anger toward me. Next he colored his dad, then his brother, his sister and himself. When he was done he started talking to me. Once the emotions were on the page, we could address his concerns and needs in a positive way.

Today's Dare
I dare you to believe that simple activities can create great breakthroughs.
In addition...

Next time you are feeling intense emotions, I dare you to grab a paper and some crayons and scribble your emotions out on the page. It's best to use fat crayons because you will be scribbling hard and they stand up to the pressure better. When you feel the emotion subsiding, color just a little longer, and then see if you can articulate your feelings to a trusted friend, therapist or your journal. If you really want to fight the negative beliefs that make you feel bad, fight them with positive affirmations while you are in the moment of emotion. This takes a lot of courage and strength, but you can do it. Everything you need is within you.

Dare 26: Symbolism of Desires

*"Symbolism is no mere idle fancy or corrupt egerneration:
It is inherent in very texture of human life."*
~*Alfred North Whitehead*

"Nature speaks in symbols and in signs."
~*John Greenleaf Whittier*

I used to want to live in the country. For years, it dominated as a key desire of mine, until one day I realized that it wasn't really the country for which I longed. It was what the country symbolized that drew me. I wanted freedom. I wanted independence. I wanted stillness. I wanted a sense of purpose. I wanted space. I wanted escape. I wanted to connect with God. For some reason, I thought I could only have those things, in the way I wanted them, if I moved to the country.

It turns out that I like living in the suburbs. I like the convenience of stores close by and people around me. Some of the most wonderful people I've ever known have been neighbors who lived right next door or across the street from me. These people helped me when I needed it, and served my family in so many ways because they were so close in proximity.

Desires are an interesting and perplexing thing. Sometimes we think we know what we want, but it's possible that sometimes the things we think we want are simply symbols of some greater, deeper longing. Once you know what you really want, what your core desire is, you then become empowered to make it a reality. I have found the freedom I was seeking, and I am finding it at greater levels every day. I have found independence, and it feels good, but it looks different than I thought. I find stillness whenever I seek it and make it happen. I feel a great sense of purpose in my life. I have all the space I need, as I create it. I have escaped those things I wanted to escape, and learned a tremendous amount along the way. I connect with God every time

I seek Him. And I did all these things without ever moving to the country!

Today's Dare

I dare you to consider that some of your desires could really be symbols for something deeper.

In addition. . .

In your journal, list at least one of your long-term desires that you haven't yet obtained. What are the deeper values that this desire symbolizes for you? Is it the desire itself or the values that you are drawn to more? What is it you really want? Can you get it in another way if you realize, like I did, that the desire isn't really your goal?

Dare 27: Gratitude

"Gratitude is not only the greatest of virtues, but the parent of all the others."
~Marcus Tillius Cicero

"There is no such thing as gratitude unexpressed. If it is unexpressed, it is plain, old-fashioned ingratitude."
~Robert Brault

Gratitude is a powerful tool for cultivating self-love. When we begin to see and appreciate the things we have, the things we lack seem less prominent.

When I personally express appreciation to God or other people in my life, I can't help but feel blessed. It's hard to be negative and depressed when you feel grateful. Gratitude is a transcendent feeling. It moves the spirit beyond the mere physical into a higher plane of thinking and feeling, a plane more aligned with the true self. If you want to know who you really are try cultivating a deep sense of gratitude.

There is extreme beauty in expressions of gratitude, whether written, spoken or felt. That beauty radiates on the countenance. The cultivation of gratitude pays profound dividends.

Today's Dare

I dare you to start keeping a gratitude journal. Decide how many things you will list each day and then write them in your journal every morning or night, whichever works best for you. As you begin to see your blessings, you will begin to feel more love for yourself, and others. Don't just limit your view of blessings as things external to you. List the good qualities about yourself that you see, too. In fact, I dare you write at least one thing on your list each day that is about yourself.

Dare 28: Creation and Creativity

"You must not for one instant give up the effort to build new lives for yourselves. Creativity means to push open the heavy, groaning doorway to life. This is not an easy struggle. Indeed, it may be the most difficult task in the world, for opening."
~Daisaku Ikeda

"Creativity is inventing, experimenting, growing, taking risks, breaking rules, making mistakes and having fun."
~Mary Lou Cook

To create simply means to bring something into existence that did not exist before. So bringing order to a room where it did not exist before is a creative act. Yes, housework is creative! Every act is a creative act, so every single one of us on the planet is creative. We are the creators of our world, vast and immediate. When we understand that everything we do is an act of creation, we begin to make more deliberate choices about what we want to be responsible for creating.

Beyond creating through words, thoughts and choices, we create through hobbies, activities, etc. One of my favorite and most therapeutic forms of creation always has been songwriting. When I have an emotion to process, I often do it through song. It allows me to more fully express what I'm feeling.

The traditional fine arts can be very therapeutic. A person can color, paint, write music, sing, sculpt, or dance at any level as a form of therapy that can be very beneficial for processing emotions. Other forms of creation, as long as you enjoy what you are doing, can serve the same purpose. It really comes down to your intention. If you are creating a masterpiece, then you have certain guidelines to follow in the creative process. If you are creating to release or process emotions, your intention will be very different and your outcome won't be hampered by standards or technique.

Expressing oneself creatively is an act of power. If you are not actively expressing yourself in creative ways (and not just through fine arts), I highly recommend you find a way to incorporate some creative time into your regular routine. You will come to know and love yourself on a deeper level as you intentionally create in a way that feels authentic to you.

Today's Dare
I dare you to believe that you are creative.
In addition . . .

I dare you to reflect on this past week. What kinds of mundane activities have you participated in that were really acts of creation? Did you think of them as creative acts? Or burdens? Have you spent any time in deliberate creativity doing something you love? If you have not, set aside some time for this purpose. Self-expression (the very essence of creativity) is essential to health and well-being. Stifling personal expression compounds problems. Let your spirit express its essence and feel the difference in your life.

Dare 29: Question Power

*"If you want to change your life, change your questions.
If you want a great life, ask great questions!"*
~ Wendy Watson Nelson

"To solve any problem, here are three questions to ask yourself: First, what could I do? Second, what could I read? And third, who could I ask?"
~Jim Rohn

One of the most helpful habits a person can develop is the ability to ask themselves meaningful and thought-provoking questions. Questions aid awareness and foster a tremendous amount of personal power. A lack of personal power is usually preceded by poor questions.

I'm sure you've noticed that almost every Dare has included questions to ponder and answer. That's because questions are so important. They lead to answers and solutions and ultimately, to self-love.

When we act from a place of habit and reaction, we tend to ask questions we can't answer. Most of those questions begin with the word "why?" Questions like, "Why did this happen to me?" leave us feeling lost, stuck and helpless because we usually can't answer them. Once we start living from a place of awareness, we can begin to ask empowering questions. Questions like, "How can I . . . ?" are especially helpful because they set our brain on a quest for solutions.

Other great questions to use for personal power:

- What am I to learn from this?
- How can I benefit from this situation, problem, or circumstance?
- What can I do differently?
- What haven't I tried?
- Who do I know that can help me?

Dare 29: Question Power

Today's Dare

I dare you to think about your questions. What kind of questions do you ask yourself? Do you ask a lot of *why?* Questions? Or more empowering questions? What is one question you can ask yourself today that can help shed new light on a problem you've been struggling with for some time? Ask a different question, get a different answer.

Dare 30: Whose Fault Is It?

"I am never a failure until I begin blaming others."
~Unknown

"The final forming of a person's character lies in their own hands."
~Anne Frank

In Dare 29, we talked about the power of questions, which is a natural lead-in to today's dare. However, this is a tough topic and some people may not be ready for it at this point in the challenge. At some stage in your journey though, I recommend incorporating this principle into your life. It will give you so much personal power and increase your capacity to make conscious choices. It will open you to greater growth and accelerate your healing journey.

The topic is personal accountability. I can only touch on this principle here; I can't possibly cover every nuance, so if you have questions, a therapist would be a great person to help you delve into this topic.

I once had an experience with a woman who pulled up some horrible feelings within me. I wrote her an email explaining how she upset me. She wrote back explaining her view of the communication and then invited me to examine my own conduct and feelings to determine my part in creating the situation. At first, I was offended that she'd turn the situation back on me. How dare she say I was to blame! But then I started thinking about it and the truth was she hadn't excused herself from blame. She had merely invited me to join her in accepting accountability for my own part in how the scene had played out.

After examining and seeing what I had done to create the situation with her, I realized this wasn't the first time I had experienced these horrible feelings. As I realized how I had "prepared the soil" so to speak, I was suddenly awakened. I recognized a pattern of emotional reaction and understood I would never have to experience that type of situation again if I didn't want to because I had been educated by personal accountability. It was a choice! Suddenly, I was very grateful to this woman for asking me to open my eyes and be humble enough to embrace power. Because that's what personal accountability is—power.

It's funny how often things in this world appearing to be weakness are actually the roots of true strength. Humans naturally tend to point the finger when something has gone wrong. We have an emotional reaction to something outside of ourselves and then place blame on whatever triggered that reaction. Yes, it may very well be someone else's fault that something happened to cause you to feel the way you do. But when you blame and point the finger—placing all the responsibility on another individual or circumstance—you lose personal power. In essence, by putting it outside of yourself, you give your power to that person or situation. You become a victim.

Blame is a chain that keeps us locked to the very thing we wish we could escape. Feelings of anger and sadness are natural and a normal part of the grieving process when something bad happens. Though these feelings should be felt, hanging onto them for too long sucks our vitality and keeps us stagnant.

One person hurt me repeatedly for years and I blamed that person for everything negative in my life. It was their fault I was unhappy because they told me I was incompetent, insecure, and ugly. This kept me weak, unhappy and stuck. The truth is I believed this person's words and that's where I needed to become accountable. No, it wasn't right or fair for them to treat me poorly, but I was accountable for believing their words. It was my choice to believe them. It took me a long time to understand that. When I finally, truly learned the principle of accountability, and that I had a choice in the matter, I was freed. I could say "That's your stuff and this is mine." Accountability keeps each player's "stuff" in their own court.

"But what is my stuff?" You ask.

Any emotions resulting as part of the situation are yours, either negative or positive. Situations and events are merely stimuli that trigger emotion. No one can place a particular emotion inside of you. It originates with you and you alone. What you do with those emotions is yours. Whether you forgive is yours. Whether you allow yourself to learn from a situation is yours. Whether you grow from the situation is yours. Seeing your part in how the situation was created is yours. Unless you are a victim of rape or abuse, which you did not create, you have a choice. And even then, you have the choice to heal.

Recently I spoke to a group of youth and parents at a program run by a local police department. After my presentation, a girl about seventeen walked up to me with her father and shared that she had been raped. She then told me that my explanation about choice and accountability had helped her see how the anger and resentment she was feeling were cankering her, keeping her miserable and stuck in unhappiness. "I now know I have a choice," she said. "I can let it go and move on."

Accountability is a hard place to come to, but this girl was ready. For many of us, we resist accountability because we think it means we are weak or at fault or broken. Sometimes we think it means we are absolving other parties from their part in the matter. On the contrary, ownership of your part and your emotions brings a tremendous amount of personal power to you and leaves others to resolve their own emotions and contributions to the problem on their own.

A person must also be aware that they can take on too much accountability by carrying other people's burdens for them. This is a form of co-dependency and should be addressed to create healthy relating habits. It's important to address accountability in a healthy way.

Today's Dare
I dare you to believe that accountability is actually true power.
In addition . . .

If you are ready to undertake the development of personal accountability, I dare you to look at a negative emotion you have toward a situation and ask yourself how you played a part in creating it. For example, if your friends have disowned you, did you do anything that could have caused that situation to manifest? Did you subconsciously desire that consequence? Did you need a change? Or are your friends simply exercising their power of choice in immature ways? If so, perhaps you're lucky to have the opportunity to move on and find new friends.

Personal accountability is recognizing when you've made choices that created a consequence. Owning those consequences and moving forward will empower you. Rather than feeling rejected, you could recognize that it was a choice and act to make things different within you. I say different within you because you may not be able to change things around you, but you can always control and change your inner world. Peace can be found amidst the chaos if you seek it. Accountability is one avenue for that.

Dare 31: Order

"I learned that we can do anything, but we can't do everything . . . at least not at the same time. So think of your priorities not in terms of what activities you do, but when you do them. Timing is everything."
~Dan Millman

I'm a very mood-driven person. I like to do what I feel like, when I feel like it. Unfortunately, I've learned this is a very frustrating way to live. It's great for spontaneity, but it doesn't work too well for accomplishing goals and living from a centered and orderly place. I've had to learn self-discipline, BUT I have been rewarded for it. There is a great energy, passion and power that come from living an ordered life. Not necessarily rigid, just ordered.

For example, review the two following summer mornings:

Morning A:
5:45 a.m. – Get up and drive my son to cheer practice.
6:00 a.m. – Study from my core religious text, write in my journal, and ponder on self-improvement, goals, responsibilities and other issues.
7:30 a.m. – Exercise.
8:00 a.m. – Shower, groom.
8:30 a.m. – Breakfast, light house work.
9:00 a.m. – Ready to tackle work, errands, time with kids, etc.

Morning B:
5:45 a.m. – Roll out of bed to drive my son to cheer practice.
6:00 a.m. – Crash back into bed and fall asleep.
8:30 a.m. – Wake up, make breakfast (because the kids are already up).
9:00 a.m. – Try to study core spiritual text through constant distractions and interruptions.
9:15 a.m. – Shower (no time to exercise), groom, light house work.
11:00 a.m. – Ready to work, run errands, etc.

Though there's only about a two-hour difference between the point where I'm fully ready to tackle my day on each morning, *Day A* is incredibly empowering for me. If I get those two quiet hours to study, exercise and get showered and dressed before the kids get up, it makes all the difference to my world. If I start my day with order, I have so much more peace in every aspect of my life. For me, order looks like *Day A*.

I charge my batteries through taking care of myself first. I know I need quiet time, alignment with God, and exercise. If I do those three things first in the morning, I feel super-charged and amazing the entire rest of the day. Problems don't seem as difficult to face. I have more time and feel less rushed and stressed.

Just like having order in the home creates an atmosphere of peace, creating order within our minds and bodies creates peace and power. How do you create order in your body and mind? You discover what you need to feel amazing and then you make it a priority. You do it first every day. Everything else falls into its proper place when you feel great and put the most important things first. Feeding your body, mind and spirit is self-love in action.

Today's Dare
I dare you to identify whether or not you are living a life of order. In addition. . . .

What do you need to feel great each day? Do you know? I dare you to find out how you can create more order in your home, mind, body and spirit and then do it!! Shift your schedule around to make time for your greatest priorities regarding self and see if you don't notice a difference in how you feel and how you handle each day. It may be a sacrifice at first, but the payoff is well worth it.

Dare 32: Physical Beauty

"For every beauty there is an eye somewhere to see it."
~Ivan Panin

*"Though we travel the world over to find the beautiful,
we must carry it with us or we find it not."*
~Ralph Waldo Emerson

I've put off addressing physical beauty till now because learning to love yourself and seeing your true beauty is a process that occurs from the inside out. Still, the physical aspect of beauty is important because it does directly affect how we feel inside. The trick is to not let the physical aspect become the sole source of confidence. Like it or not, none of us is immune to aging. Physical beauty fades, but true inner beauty is lasting.

Unfortunately, society emphasizes external beauty so much for commercial profit that we can have a very hard time separating our self-worth from the indoctrination we have received about beauty. We must retrain our thoughts and beliefs about what makes us beautiful as girls, as women. Part of that retraining is recognizing and maximizing what we have been physically blessed with. When a woman takes care of, and optimizes the outside, she feels good inside. Likewise, when she takes care of, and maximizes the inside, she feels good on the outside. Both must be addressed.

If there is an aspect of the external self that makes you unhappy, then work to change it if you can. If there's an aspect of the external self you can't change, then work to change the inside—your beliefs, thoughts and associations regarding that aspect. It can be done. I've done it. When I couldn't get plastic surgery, I wondered how I could ever love myself or think I was pretty. As I worked on the inside, over time, those feelings changed and I was able to love myself and see myself as beautiful. And because I had made internal changes that strengthened my character, I became more of a woman of substance with more to offer others.

You can't lose when you learn to love yourself, but it is unwise to neglect outer beauty in this process. Take the time to learn how to apply makeup properly, or to dress in a way that makes you feel good and shows respect for others. Standing up straight, smiling, or getting a haircut that makes you look and feel fabulous are all part of the process. Each aspect adds to the whole. It's worthwhile to assess where you can improve your physical beauty, but it is important to balance those assessments with the inner self and keep physical beauty in perspective. In other words, don't make it all about the body and the face, but do what you can with what you've been blessed with.

Today's Dare
I dare you to think of beauty as a holistic experience,
Not just a physical experience.
In addition...

Do you feel good about yourself physically? What aspects of your physical appearance can you control? Which aspects can you not control? What can you do about each of these things? What prevents you from making changes? Health problems? Thought and belief patterns? I dare you to gently assess yourself and determine where you can make one small shift in the way you care for your physical body that will help you feel more beautiful physically.

Dare 33: Fear vs. Courage

"Courage is reckoned the greatest of all virtues; because, unless a man has that virtue, he has no security for preserving any other".
~Samuel Johnson

"Courage doesn't always roar. Sometimes courage is the little voice at the end of the day that says I'll try again tomorrow."
~Mary Anne Radmacher

There's a story I love. It's about a woman who, during the Revolutionary War era, had to make a sudden decision—face death—to save her son's life. At this pivotal moment, she first shrank from the task, but within seconds, a surge of conviction coursed through her veins sending her courageously to save the life of her son and nine other boys. She was simply a housewife who had no idea that she possessed the heroic capacity to save lives. I'm sure it never occurred to her as she went about her daily chores and responsibilities that she would have the courage to demand the release of her young kidnapped son at knife point and succeed.

Generally, we don't have courage until courage is required. When I competed in my first pageant, I didn't think I had the courage to face the judgments of 700 people, a video camera taping the whole thing and five tough judges, but I did. And I survived!!! That act alone paid huge dividends in my healing process, my confidence level, and the knowledge that I can do hard things.

The opposite of courage is fear. Fear is what keeps us stuck where we are. It takes tremendous courage to look inside our hearts, see the mess, accept accountability for our part in that mess, and then clean it up. If you are embarking on this path of heart-cleaning you are one of the most courageous people I know. Most people don't go there, not because they lack the courage, but because they give into fear.

I recently watched the movie *The Green Lantern*. The creature that represented fear in the movie grew to greater and greater proportions as it fed on itself. It was only destroyed as courage was embraced and fear was faced. As Emerson said, "Do the thing you fear and death of fear is certain."

My favorite book is *The Hiding Place* by Corrie Ten Boom. At one point in the book, she speaks of her youth and her first encounter with death, that of a neighbor's child. At that moment, she realized that the people in her family, the people she loved most, could die. She told her father she didn't think she had the strength to face it if he died. Her wise father said, "When the time comes that some of us will have to die, you will look into your heart and find the strength you need, just in time."

And so it is with us. We find courage and strength as we need it, in the measure we need it, and at the time we need it. And we always find just enough to get through, even when it feels like we won't make it. It is in the reaching, the stretching of self, that we grow in strength, love and confidence. Each act of courage conquers a measure of fear. As we persist in courageous acts, especially ones like heart healing, we change the world. For as we change ourselves, we cannot help but change everything we touch.

Today's Dare

I dare you to remind yourself that you are courageous. In fact I dare you to state the following affirmations:

I AM courageous.

Between me and my Higher Power I have all the resources I need to face and defeat my fears with courage.

Dare 34: Self-Betrayal

*"How desperately difficult it is to be honest with oneself.
It is much easier to be honest with other people."*
~Edward Frederic Benson

"The most common form of despair is not being who you are."
~Soren Kierkegaard

I used to do it all the time. I still do it sometimes. But now, I usually catch myself, and if I don't catch myself in the act, I know immediately after that I've done it because I feel it.

What am I talking about?

Self-betrayal.

Self-betrayal is that feeling you get when you know you shouldn't do something, when you know you should say "no," or when you know you should honor your inner wisdom and you don't. Beyond that, self-betrayal is any act that keeps us from living at our highest level. Self-betrayal leads to guilt and frustration which then leave us trying to justify our actions with excuses to soothe that guilt away. The practice of self-betrayal is the practice of living a lie. It dishonors the true self and weakens boundaries. Most of us practice self-betrayal in minimal amounts, but self-betrayal is a robber and a thief of personal power and joy.

So what's the solution to self-betrayal? Again, the answer comes down to awareness and humility. The awareness to recognize what is going on and the willingness (humility) to recognize ways in which you might be betraying yourself. As we accept accountability for the self-betrayal we have practiced, we are then empowered to make different choices that strengthen, rather than weaken, the self.

In my marriage, I betrayed myself for years. I tried to change who I was to please my spouse for whom I never seemed to be good enough. As I lost more and more of who I was through self-betrayal, I began to hate myself and experience tremendous confusion about what I wanted to do with my life, what my purpose was and what I was supposed to be doing. I could never seem to get any clear direction, which confused me even more. But how could I possibly find any answers about my life when I was constantly denying my true identity? It's wasn't possible. I had to reclaim myself, stop the self-betrayal, and own who I was. Once that process of reclamation hit a climax, and I was strong enough to be me despite anyone else's opinions, only then could I address the hard questions and decisions of how to honor myself at the highest level. For me, that meant divorce. The point is, I was finally empowered enough to make those choices and answer those questions.

Loving myself enough to own who I am despite my imperfections has literally changed my life. There is power in self-ownership, self-love. It unleashes a host of strengths you didn't even know you had, but it takes consistent work and pure desire to overcome self-betrayal and other self-defeating behaviors. The question is: What will you give, or sacrifice, to be free of consistent negative feelings and patterns? Will you give your pride away? Will you listen to your true self? Will you give away self-betrayal?

An excellent book on the many faces of self-betrayal is *Bonds that Make Us Free* by C. Terry Warner. I highly recommend this book addressing self-betrayal in the individual and how it affects our relationships.

Today's Dare

I dare you to consider the ways in which you might be betraying yourself. Write down the biggest way(s) in which you practice self-betrayal. Why do you do it? Is it to please others? Is it to bring others down so you can feel justified in some way? Is it to keep yourself feeling down because you don't believe you deserve to feel good? Some other reason? You are not your self-betrayal. Who you are at the core is beauty and light. Ownership of that light and beauty is your true power. I dare you to shed, inch by inch, your self-betraying tendencies (because we all have them to some degree), and own who you are.

Dare 35: Basic Body Language

"I speak two languages, body and English."
~Mae West

"The universal principle of etymology in all languages: words are carried over form bodies and from the properties of bodies to express the things of he mind and spirit. The order of ideas must follow the order of things."
~Giambattista Vico

One physical aspect of confidence and self-love is the way you carry yourself. Do you slouch? Do you make eye contact with others? Do you smile? All of these things make a difference, not only in how you appear to others, but also in how you feel about yourself. If I'm standing up straight not only do I feel more confident, I look more confident. Slouching communicates "shrinking away from" and "don't approach me" in body language. Standing up straight implies that you know and are comfortable with who you are and with others.

When I first committed to doing a pageant, one of the very first things I did was start standing up straighter. It took a little while to get used to but it was worth it. I felt better about myself and how I appeared to others.

A smile communicates friendliness, openness and approachability to other people. To the self, it communicates good feelings. Eye contact does the same. Both are habits worth developing.

Your mind believes your body and your body believes your mind. What messages are you sending it by the way you hold yourself and the facial expressions you wear and share with others? These seem like small things but they really make a difference in how you feel and how others feel about you.

Today's Dare

I dare you to notice the way you carry yourself or communicate through body language. Are these ways invalidating? Do they send negative messages to yourself and others? Try sitting up straight and smiling when you feel down. Mood is affected by physiology and vice versa.

Dare 36: Life Vision

"The vision that you glorify in your mind, the ideal that you enthrone in your heart, this you will build your life by, and this you will become".
~Anonymous

"Where there is no vision the people perish."
~Proverbs 29:18

Do you have a life vision?

I knew what I wanted to do when I was 15 years old. I kept seeing myself doing certain things and feeling deep inexplicable desires toward these "visions of possibility." As I got older and fell deeper and deeper into the loss of self, they seemed more and more impossible to achieve. I blocked the possibility of their manifestation because I didn't know how they could ever come to pass. Eventually, I got to the point where I didn't know what I was supposed to be doing with my life. I felt utter confusion. Truth is, I knew. I just couldn't believe it for myself, but as I have recovered self-worth and learned to love myself, the same old desires and longings from when I was young have returned.

About two years ago, I finally wrote out a life vision for myself. As I have gained clarity about my purpose and desires, the vision has changed slightly, but it has given me something toward which to work. Writing a life vision helped me define my desires and goals at the time and was helpful in uncovering my truth. I have had to rewrite my life vision because there have been some major shifts in my life. Also, I realized that some of my desires were symbolic (like wanting to live way out in the country somewhere). Some things I thought I wanted and were important just aren't anymore. And that's okay. You always can rework your life vision at any time.

A life vision brings meaning and purpose to life. It helps you feel directed and reminds you what you are trying to achieve out of life. It's very easy to forget our dreams and what is truly important in life because we get caught up in the hustle and bustle of everyday living.

Ann Webb (www.ideallifevision.com) offers services that help you create a life vision and provides a way to "imprint" it on your subconscious. *Designing Your Life Vision* by Karen Poole also is a great book that takes you through the process of life visioning creatively. Perfect for those who like to scrapbook or get crafty.

Another great way to keep track of what you want to achieve in life is a Bucket List. A Bucket List is much quicker to write out than a life vision and less specific. I have both. It's a good place to start if you're not ready to tackle a life vision. Google "Bucket List Ideas" to find and follow bucket lists of other people for some great inspiration. As you read other peoples' lists, you'll see things you didn't even realize you wanted to do. It's kind of fun!

Today's Dare

If you don't already have one, start a Bucket List or begin jotting down ideas for your life vision. Address spirituality, relationships, vocation, physical environment, emotional goals, creativity, and lifestyle. When you write your plan, write it as if you have already achieved it in present tense. Describe how you feel, what you see, hear, smell, and taste. This makes the process highly sensory and impactful. When you complete your vision, read it out loud daily. I dare you.

Dare 37: Nourishment

"If we could give every individual the right amount of nourishment and exercise, not too little and not too much, we would have found the safest way to health."
~Hippocrates

"Health requires healthy food."
~Roger Williams

The dictionary defines nourishment as follows:

- To sustain with food or nutriment; supply with what is necessary for life, health, and growth.
- To cherish, foster, keep alive, etc.
- To strengthen, build up, or promote

Most of us are pretty good at nourishing ourselves in a way that keeps us alive, but are we nourishing ourselves in ways that enable us to thrive? Nourishment is more than feeding the physical body food. We must nourish our minds to keep them active and healthy. We must nourish our spirits to keep ourselves aligned and progressing. The way we nourish ourselves is an individual process based upon personal beliefs, preferences and desires.

My entire process of learning to love myself was a process of learning to nourish myself. I had to understand my needs to be able to gift myself with those things. It took time to build these new habits. It was, and still is, a continual balancing act because what I need from day to day subtly (and sometimes drastically) changes as my life shifts. The key is flexibility. Recognizing the need to nourish body, mind and spirit and then following through on the things we discover as we uncover them is crucial. Stress accumulates and drains life and light from us. Conscious nourishment is essential to confidence, health and happiness.

Dare 37: Nourishment

Today's Dare

I dare you to ask yourself: Am I nourishing my body? My mind? My spirit? In what ways? Write in your journal at least one way you can nourish each of these areas. If you aren't sure what would be most beneficial to you, be still and listen to your heart. What do you discover there? What does it mean to you to nourish yourself? What makes you feel nourished? Is there some specific way you receive nourishment from yourself? From others? Are you getting it in healthy ways? If not, do you know why you receive it the way you do? Is there another, healthier, way you could receive it? Explore these questions. I dare you.

Dare 38: Solutions

"As long as anyone believes that his ideal and purpose is outside him, that it is above the clouds, in the past or in the future, he will go outside himself and seek fulfillment
where it cannot be found. He will look for solutions and answers at every point except where they can be found—in himself."
~Erich Fromm

Early in my healing process, I wrote a helpful exercise in my journal. I listed my biggest problems and then categorized each one as an "obstacle." A problem requires solving. An obstacle is a block that needs to be worked around. It's just a slightly different way of viewing a challenge. Sometimes the way we label something can hinder us or help us. Where we may not be able to find a *solution*, we might be able to find a *way around*.

After I wrote down the obstacle I was facing, I brainstormed ideas that could help me deal with each one. So instead of pressuring myself to find answers, I sought out ways to cope. Removing pressure often opens a way for answers to flow through us. Also, asking questions (like we discussed in Dare 29) can help lead to new ideas or "ways around" that we might not have thought of before.

Another thing I've uncovered in connection with seeking solutions is the tendency to make excuses. This brings us back to awareness of thought processes. I noticed a pattern within myself. Whenever I hit on a possible answer or way around my problem, I rationalized why I couldn't pursue it. What I came to realize was that those were the very ideas I needed to explore further. However, I wasn't ready or willing to do what was required to reap the benefits of such a solution, so I made excuses. Until I realized what was going on, it was an involuntary and subconscious process. Those excuses only kept me stuck in places I didn't want to be and locked in feelings I didn't want to have. Again, it comes down to Dare 1: How bad do you want it? Excuses are a red flag that you might be onto something that you probably should explore further.

Dare 38: Solutions

Today's Dare

I dare you to write a list in your journal of current obstacles that you're dealing with and brainstorm ideas that would help you positively deal with those obstacles. Could any of these ideas be a solution? An answer? If you find yourself making excuses about why you can't really pursue any of these positive ideas, consider the reason why. What is holding you back from moving forward?

Dare 39: Rhythm

"Action and reaction, ebb and flow, trial and error, change - this is the rhythm of living."
~Bruce Barton

"Rhythm is the basis of life, not steady forward progress."
~Kabbalah

When I went to Maui two years ago, I thought a lot about many aspects of my life. As I watched the waves move in and out rhythmically and felt the slower, serene pace of my days, I realized I didn't like the rhythm of my life back home. Certainly home life has a much different pace than vacation that, realistically, can't be adopted. Of course I couldn't do the same things at home I did on vacation. I couldn't spend countless hours basking in the sun at the beach or bumming around and spending money without working to replenish it. But I could adopt a different mindset, I could slow things down.

As a songwriter I liken life pace to a song. Each song has a rhythm that determines the overall feel and mood created for the listener. Likewise, our lives have a rhythm, created by our thoughts, choices and actions that combine to create a feel—an overall rhythm—for our days. If I have stressful, pressured, or hurried thought patterns, I will feel, and likely live, a stressful, pressured, hurried life pace. If I want a slower rhythm, I must learn to slow my thought patterns. That doesn't mean I have racing thoughts. It means I may have too many thoughts, too many commitments, running through my head at the same time, all vying for attention. This can create a sense of "I need to hurry and get this and that done." If you listen to an upbeat song constantly it gets tiring. Everyone needs down time. If life is constantly like an accelerated Techno song, it will wear on you after a while.

If you find that you can never relax and always feel bogged down with too much to do, it may be time to analyze your life rhythm and determine whether changes are in order.

How do I change my life rhythm?
Here are a few tips:

1. Make time for stillness as discussed in Dare 20.
2. Learn to say NO.
3. Analyze your priorities and stick to your boundaries as described in Dare 23.
4. Breathe, as detailed in Dare 8.
5. Decide what you want to experience and commit to creating it.

Today's Dare

I dare you to look at the pace of your life and decide if you are happy with it. If you are, great! If not, consider why. What is it about the pace you're living you don't like? Look at your thought patterns for clues. What choices are you making that develop and support the life pace you are living? Explore these things in your journal. Introduce small changes into your life where you can.

Dare 40: Self-Expression

"Self-expression must pass into communication for its fulfillment."
~Pearl S. Buck

"No man has the right to dictate what other men should perceive, create or produce, but all should be encouraged to reveal themselves, their perceptions and emotions, and to build confidence in the creative spirit."
~Ansel Adams

The process of learning to love yourself is really a process of learning to find your voice, the unique, confident way in which you express yourself and gift the world.

Self-expression is not just an end, it is a means that can and should be used throughout the entire journey of life. On my personal journey, I have used many forms of self-expression and for many reasons:

- As a form of therapy to help me work through and process emotions, I often write songs.
- To develop skills. At one point, I learned to draw and that helped me develop an eye for, and attention to, detail.
- To balance the concrete and abstract in my life. Sometimes I prefer to take photos or paint, rather than write. All are forms of communication, but painting and photography are more symbolic and abstract while writing is more specific and concrete. Sometimes, I just need to express myself in different ways.
- To discover new talents and abilities.

Exploration is a gift. So what if you try something new and you stink at it? Does that mean you are a failure? No. As you try new things and improve, you gain confidence in new areas. Confidence fuels self-love. As we come to see and understand what we are capable of and the gifts we embody, the seed of confidence is planted.

I remember when I tried out for cheerleading my freshman year of high school. I stunk so badly. I really can't believe I even made the squad, but I quickly discovered I had a talent for dance, formations and routines. By the end of the year, I was quite good. I gained confidence in my abilities as my skills grew. I never would have discovered this passion for dance had I not summoned the courage to try.

Self-expression is important in the process of releasing emotional garbage, but we tend to get stuck in patterns of self-expression. For example, if talking with your girlfriends and receiving their validation about your problems works as your mode of self-expression, then you will likely continue to do it. The problem is that talking endlessly about problems might make you feel better in the moment but it doesn't DO anything about them. It's important to use other activities you enjoy, or to which you feel drawn, to help you release and process emotions too.

Today's Dare

Write in your journal a list of ways you cope or process problems and emotions. What are some other ways that you could balance what you're already doing? For example, if you use words a lot, what are some non-word activities through which you can channel your energy? Sports? Dance? Painting? Sewing? Collage? Cooking? Building things? Anything you can deliberately do to process emotions can benefit you. Not only do these activities serve as a release, but they also help develop you as a person and build confidence. Try at least one new activity this week.

Dare 41: Freedom

"Freedom is never voluntarily given by the oppressor; it must be demanded by the oppressed."
~Martin Luther King, Jr.

"Freedom makes a huge requirement of every human being. With freedom comes responsibility. For the person who is unwilling to grow up, the person who does not want to carry his own weight, this is a frightening prospect."
~Eleanor Roosevelt

Freedom, sweet freedom.

I have known my share of personal prisons. In one way or another, I think we all have. My greatest prison, shared in this book, was the prison of my beliefs about who I was and what I could accomplish. I couldn't be or do any of the things I wanted to because I hated myself and believed the negative things others said about my abilities and potential. I was a wreck and couldn't see how to get out. I felt trapped.

Since that time, I have discovered two secrets to feeling personal freedom in life:

1. Authenticity– Once I was able to accept myself for who I was, I was able to BE who I was. When we stop worrying what others think and embrace who we are, flaws and all, we become authentic. Authenticity breeds freedom. Liberation from the fear of rejection is freedom.

2. Release– Accepting my situation and the responsibility that I could make changes from within, and then deciding and acting upon those changes brought release. Release is letting go of habits, thoughts, beliefs or anything negative that keeps you stuck. Once I let go of the garbage in my heart, I finally had the power to change my physical environment through divorce. I just couldn't do that until I had resolved my inner issues. I had to know that my decision was clear and based on sound judgment, not emotion. Others

may not be able to get clear until they remove themselves from a bad situation, or make changes in their physical environment. It's a very personal process and decision. Once I did the hard work, made the hard decisions, and moved forward, freedom followed quickly.

Taking the Dares in this book will help you walk through some of the process of learning to love yourself, to release old patterns and be authentic. Ultimately though, you are accountable for the results you get because they are based on your actions. Don't give up on yourself and your efforts if freedom doesn't come quickly, or in the way or shape you anticipated. Be persistent. America's forefathers didn't gain freedom in the blink of an eye. They had to fight for it. So do we. It just looks different when the battleground is the heart. Hang in there and fight. When you finally win, it's worth more than gold.

Today's Dare

Consider ways in which you might be more authentic in your life. Are you living in accordance with your values, desires and Higher Power? Are you taking opportunities and making consistent efforts to release old, unhealthy habits? What does freedom look like to you? Feel like? Journal about freedom. Paint a picture with words, in present tense, about the freedom you enjoy as you love yourself and embrace authenticity and practices of release.

Dare 42: Social Interaction

"The art of being yourself at your best is the art of unfolding your personality into the [wo]man you want to be. Be gentle with yourself, learn to love yourself, to forgive yourself,
for only as we have the right attitude toward ourselves can we have the right attitude toward others."
~Wilfred Peterson

You may already be a social person, but what is the quality and type of your social interaction? I'd invite you to explore the ways you socialize. Ask yourself a few questions:

- Does my social sphere extend beyond my best friends? Do I stick to a small, familiar group of people? Or do I regularly meet new people?
- Do I interact with many different age groups on a regular basis?
- When I interact with others, are my communications uplifting and mature, or shallow, gossipy and/or degrading to myself or others?
- What activities do I engage in when I socialize?
- Do any of my efforts include serving others? Serving others is more than just feeding and clothing the less fortunate. Using gifts and talents to uplift is service.
- Would I say that the majority of my social interactions are positive?

I used to keep my social circles pretty limited. I met people, but very slowly and I was very guarded because I was so insecure and afraid of rejection. As I began to heal myself and feel more love for myself, expanding my social circles came naturally and my confidence increased. The more I forgot about myself, the more quality and positive interactions I had with others, the better I felt about myself, and the more I was able to give.

When we socialize with others in positive ways, our ability to love self and others grows. This type of love increases confidence. When you give to another, through words or action, you strengthen your character, and confidence can't help but flow through you.

Today's Dare

I dare you to address the above questions in your journal. Also, how can you improve the quality of your social interactions? Do you notice any patterns in your interactions that either add to, or detract from, your self-worth, confidence or feelings of beauty and love? Can any of those negative interactions be replaced with more positive ones? Where do you feel comfortable? Small groups? Big groups? Older people? Younger people? Why? Are you intimidated or inhibited in some way? Or do you gravitate to those groups because you have inherent gifts that are drawn out by that groups' energy?

Dare 43: Beauty Hunt

"I've never seen a smiling face that was not beautiful."
~Author Unknown

"That which is striking and beautiful is not always good, but that which is good is always beautiful."
~Ninon de L'Enclos

We did a belief hunt on beauty back on Dare 11. In this Dare, we're going to do something a little different with the topic of beauty. We are going to look at the whole self and acknowledge the intrinsic beauty you possess.

Take out your journal and write down every attribute you possess: physical, emotional, character, and spiritual, that is beautiful about you. DO NOT use cultural or media definitions of beauty as comparisons while you write your list. Instead, look for the things you consider beautiful. If I went by the ideal of perfect facial proportions, my eyes might be considered too close set, but despite their proximity to one another, they are a deep brown and I have decently long eyelashes. So, I might write that my eyes are soulful. I might write that I have soft skin. I might write that I'm loving or compassionate. I might include that I have integrity. All these things contribute to my overall beauty and worth as a woman.

Today's Dare

Time to look at yourself. I dare you to write as fast as you can and list as many things about yourself as you can that are beautiful. Don't second guess or judge what comes up. Just write. When you can't write anymore, look in the mirror to find any additional things to add to your list. Also, think of compliments other people have given you and write those down as well. Don't focus solely on the physical. Beauty is more than physical features.

Dare 44: Mirroring

"The beautiful thing about learning is that nobody can take it away from you."
~B. B. King

"The only person you are destined to become is the person you decide to be."
~Ralph Waldo Emerson

People are like mirrors. They can show us things about ourselves if we let them, but it requires a certain level of maturity and the ability to accept accountability for behavior. As with any of the Dares, if you're not quite ready for this step, wait to adopt the concepts shared in this Dare, or discuss them with a therapist.

When somebody does something that bugs you, it's a good time to stop and reflect. They could be mirroring a behavior or attribute that bugs you about yourself. For example, if I said, "I hate how my sister always criticizes everyone," it may actually be that I have a problem with criticism I haven't consciously recognized, and my sister is a mirror showing me what needs to be addressed and healed within myself.

I'm not saying that every time someone does something that bugs you that it means you struggle with the same problem on a personal level. Obviously, if someone smokes and that action bugs you, but you've never even touched a cigarette, it doesn't mean you have issues to resolve with the physical act of smoking. Perhaps that behavior is simply a violation of your personal standards or values, and that's okay. We all have the right to choose our behavior, but it's worth considering that some people may be reflecting issues back at you.

Every issue you resolve within yourself brings you to a higher level of personal power and love that spills over into everything you do and everyone with whom you interact. The refinement of character is the most worthy pursuit on which you can ever embark.

How do you know if someone is a mirror?

Does their behavior annoy you, irritate you or make you angry? If so, it's time to do a little sleuthing.

Let's walk through an example:

Your sister says, "Wow, he is so stupid."

Your statement, or thought in response is, "She is so judgmental. I hate that."

You then might ask yourself, "Could I be judgmental?"

Let's twist it around and check.

"I am so judgmental. I hate that."

Your argument might be, "But I'm not. I try not to criticize others and rarely do it."

That may be true, but do you criticize yourself?

Epiphany. "Oh! I do."

Now you are empowered with knowledge. Now you can act to resolve your issue of self-judgment because you are aware of it.

Or maybe your answer is, "No. I don't judge myself."

It may be that you're just not ready to admit and deal with that fact. Or, it may very well be that you really don't have personal issues with judging self and others. So then you would ask yourself, "Why does her judgmental nature bother me?"

Consider what it is about judgment that makes you so mad? Perhaps it's a tool that's been placed within you to make positive changes in the world. Maybe you feel an injustice when others are judged wrongly or harshly. Can you take that irritation and channel it into a positive action that will bless the world in some way? Even a small way? Perhaps there are rights you could lobby for, or perhaps you could serve as an advocate for a specific group of people who suffer from judgments of some kind.

Emotions serve a purpose. They are being mirrored back to you for a reason. Something within you needs to be healed or addressed or utilized. Find out what it is and take action, whether within yourself or the world, do something about it. Remember that as you heal yourself, you heal the world, and as you heal the world, you heal yourself. Isn't that beautiful?

Today's Dare

I dare you to consider that people are mirrors who can teach you powerful things about yourself. The next time a negative emotion is triggered in you by someone else, go through the example above and see what you can uncover about yourself. An excellent resource for this kind of exploration is *Loving What Is* by Byron Katie. Remember to record your experience in your journal.

Dare 45: The Gift of You

"The only gift is a portion of thyself."
~Ralph Waldo Emerson

Today is the final Dare in the official *Love Yourself Dare* challenge. If you have incorporated any of the Dares into your life on a regular basis, you have begun to build awareness (the key to change), and you are on your way to acquiring greater self-love, confidence and, consequently, success. Remember, it is a journey worth the work required to reach the destination.

As I think about my past and as I see the ugly terrain I have crossed, I have come to recognize my journey as a gift. My experiences have shaped me and molded my character—refined me—in so many ways. They have equipped me with substance that I can now share with others. As character and confidence are strengthened, we have more to offer the world. It's a process to adopt the mindset of seeing ourselves as the gift we really are. Each person is indeed a gift, sent to bless lives, create opportunities for growth and provide conditions for us to become better people. If we could all see each other in this way, imagine what the world would be like! But it starts with our own hearts.

If you are at a point where you believe people cause pain, keep working on the Dares. Keep striving for positive change in your life and keep reaching out. Find mentors in people, books and experiences. As you increase your awareness and understanding, as you let things go, as your perceptions shift, as you begin to see yourself differently, you will begin to see others differently as well. Your whole world can change. Never stop hoping and never quit trying.

Embrace life. Embrace love. Embrace beauty.
Be you and love it!
I dare you.

The Final Dare

I dare you to accept the truth:
You Are a Gift.

I dare you to accept the truth:
Everyone is a gift.

I dare you to share who you are, your talents, abilities, strengths, and even vulnerabilities, in blessing other people's lives. I dare you to embrace who you are—to own who you are—and love yourself. Keep striving toward higher and higher levels of self-respect and love. Seek daily to discover the beauty that is yours by working to be a little better than you were the day before. Be gentle with yourself. Allow yourself to make mistakes and move forward at a realistic pace. Perseverance is what really matters.

God bless your journey, my friend. You are worth it.

~Jennifer

About the Author

Jennifer Griffiths Manges is a native of Northern California and a graduate of the New York Institute of Photography. A singer-songwriter, artist and professional photographer she loves to create and inspire through the arts. As a speaker for women and teen girls she shares messages of hope on the topics of adversity, true beauty, confidence, self-worth and positive life change. She served as Ms. Utah US Continental for the year 2011 and is currently serving as Ms. Utah US Continental 2012. Jennifer resides in Utah with her husband, three children and three step-children. *The Love Yourself Dare* is her first book.

www.TheLoveYourselfDare.com

14413727R00171

Made in the USA
Charleston, SC
09 September 2012